The
Recovery
of
Love

The *Recovery* *of* *Love*

Christian Mysticism and the Addictive Society

Jeffrey D. Imbach

CROSSROAD • NEW YORK

1992

The Crossroad Publishing Company
370 Lexington Avenue, New York, NY 10017

Printed in the United States of America
Typesetting output: TEXSource, Houston

Library of Congress Cataloging-in-Publication Data

Imbach, Jeffrey D.
    The recovery of love : Christian mysticism and the addictive
society / Jeffrey D. Imbach.
      p. cm.
    ISBN 0-8245-1189-1; 0-8245-1116-6 (pbk.)
    1. Love—Religious aspects—Christianity. 2. Mysticism—History—
Middle Ages, 600–1500. 3. Civilization, Modern—20th century.
4. Moral conditions. I. Title. II. Title: Addictive society.
BV4639.I59 1992
248.4'7—dc20
                                                    91-38164
                                                      CIP

This book is dedicated to the memory of
Sr. Nora Cummins, FCJ

with love

for believing in her own growth
into the freedom of passionate love

and

for believing in mine

Contents

Part III
JOHN RUUSBROEC
Love and Passion

Part IV
MEISTER ECKHART
Coming Home to Ourselves

Part V
DANTE ALIGHIERI
The Glory of Passionate Exchange

Foreword

The Recovery of Love is a splendid book. I am grateful for the opportunity to introduce it, not only because of my five-year friendship with its author, Jeff Imbach, but also because of having been privileged to be so close to its making.

What is this book about? It is about passion! Although the word "love" is used in many ways and in many places throughout the text, the word that is clearly closest to Jeff Imbach's heart is "passion." From my many conversations with Jeff, I know that "passion" expresses best the center of his life: his joys and his pain, his ecstasy and his agony, his hopes and his fears.

What is this book saying about passion? It says in strong but nuanced language that we don't have to police, deny, ignore or push aside our passion, but can choose to open up our passion "until it unlocks its deepest treasure, until it reveals its own eternal Source, its inherent glory." Guided by four great fourteenth-century mystics — Julian of Norwich, John Ruusbroec, Meister Eckhart, and Dante Alighieri — Jeff Imbach offers in this book a spirituality that honors our passion as the holy ground in which God's love is hidden.

Reading this book, I found myself quickly becoming a companion, yes, even a friend of these great spiritual writers from a century as tumultuous as ours. They offer me a liberating framework for my often unsettling communion with God's heart, they point out that my anxious needs can lead me to my true self, and they reveal to me that my deepest fulfilment can be found in that most human act, the act of adoration. What these great spiritual guides did for me, they certainly will also do for every passionate reader of this book.

Who is Jeff Imbach? I met Jeff for the first time in August 1986 in his hometown, Calgary, in Alberta, Canada. I vividly remember how he welcomed me and his long-time friend, Nathan Ball, at the Calgary Airport, and drove us to a small park for a picnic lunch. There we talked about his family, his ministry, his visions and his dreams.

Jeff is a warm, open man who, at times, can burst out in loud, jovial laughter. He listens with great attention and speaks with strong conviction. He makes you feel cared for, but also challenges you. He gives you much space to move, but also creates clear boundaries. He offers friendship easily and generously, but does not allow you to become dependent on him. While not afraid to put his own life on the line, he always points to something or someone far larger than himself. I know few people in whom protective closeness and freeing distance are so beautifully balanced as in Jeff Imbach. Jeff, the husband of Miriam and the father of Julie and Nikki, is a friend and minister to many. He is the pastor of Barnabas Christian Fellowship, a Christian community that seeks to be a place of refuge and healing for those who are seeking an authentic spiritual commitment within the realities of our contemporary world. He is a true bridge-builder. Being himself a layman, he builds bridges with the ordained ministry. Being himself deeply rooted in the evangelical tradition, he builds bridges with the Catholic and Anglican traditions. Being himself steeped in the Protestant work ethic, he builds bridges with the mystical spirituality. Being himself very much at home in his own time and culture, he builds bridges with the great thinkers of other times and cultures. Finally, and most of all, being very much in touch with his own and others' passion, he builds bridges with those faraway men and women who not only were well in touch with their own passions, but also had great wisdom to offer for the transformation of that passion into a splendid source of love.

This book is a wise book. Its wisdom is not a borrowed wisdom. It is a wisdom born of the personal struggles of its author, lived in the light of the Gospel of Jesus Christ, and shaped by the great mystics of the Church.

This book is also a pastoral book. Jeff Imbach is not afraid to share his own pain, nor does he hesitate to acknowledge the autobiographical nature of his writing, but he also dares to consult his brothers and sisters from far away and long ago to critically evaluate his own journey and to lift his own life far above the idiosyncrasies of his personal experiences.

Finally, this is a healing book. Our unruly passions, guilt and shame-provoking as they can be, are given back to us to be honored and claimed as the way to the place where the deepest desire of our heart is fulfilled, the place of everlasting communion.

Until the publication of this book, Jeff Imbach has been a committed pastor to the small circle of people who form the Barnabas community in Calgary, Canada. I hope and pray that this book will make him a minister also to the many people living in very different places and situations who search for ways to transform their passion into a source of unlimited love.

HENRI J. M. NOUWEN

Preface

This past fall a Native American named Austin Tootoosis spoke to our community. He recounted his own experience of oppression and his journey into healing. Part of his story is that he is a recovering alcoholic. In his recovery he has begun to rediscover his own spiritual and cultural heritage within the native tradition.

Austin's story embodies a burgeoning movement across Canada, a renaissance of Native American identity. It is not a frightened clinging to a hollow shell. Like others with him, Austin is making a life-affirming choice to bring his past with him into his present life as a part of his own healing.

Walter Brueggemann calls Christians to a similar choice in his book, *The Prophetic Imagination*.[1] He writes that if the church is going to recover its power to believe and to act, it will have to recover its communal memory.

The power to believe and act. Now that is a potent phrase! It touches a deep but often elusive longing. It implies rootedness and integration, qualities that may seem beyond us.

What might it mean to recover the communal memory? Obviously there could be myriad convergences between the memory of the community and the present. This book is about one of those convergences. It is about the vision of passionate love expressed by Julian of Norwich, John Ruusbroec, Meister Eckhart, and Dante Alighieri as that vision resonates with the contemporary chaos around intimate relationships, the deeply rooted longing for love and the journey into recovery experienced by so many today.

Our world is desperate for a positive vision, a gutsy vision of love that incorporates all of who we are — minds, bodies, and spirits. I believe there is no better place to go than to that part of our Christian tradition which saw love as the essence of our spirituality and dared to describe the outline of that vision for us. Here we are invited to reclaim the deepest truth of our passion and to become lovers — free to live with passionate integrity.

These four writers all belonged to the same chaotic fourteenth century. They lived through a cataclysmic collapse of the old and the emergence of an uncertain future. Yet none of them ended up in cynicism or despair. Each in her or his own way brought to birth, out of that time, a unique and indispensable contribution to a larger vision of love that they offer to us.

The recovery of love, then, is about our contemporary search for intimacy and about our communal memory of a full-bodied vision of passionate love.

I will not give a full introduction to any of the writers discussed in this book.[2] Those introductions are available already, and one book would be far too little space to deal with such a varied task.

It is my desire to help readers make friends with some of the great voices of the Christian tradition. These people can become true companions who speak to the very issues that make many feel so alone and lost. I offer them as soul friends to you on your own pilgrimage of faith.

Some may be enticed to go on and read these spiritual fore-mothers and forefathers. That would be the final compliment.

I am not alone in this journey. Nor are the insights here mine in any unique sense. I am deeply grateful for the encouragement of Fr. Henri Nouwen who, as a true friend, encouraged me to write when I had no courage to try. Cheryl Lee Molohon and Bonnie Tarchuck spent many hours helping me find my voice. I want to express my thanks to them and to the others who read the manuscript and offered suggestions. My thanks also goes to Robert Heller, of Crossroad/Continuum who has been a very supportive editor and guide.

I am deeply grateful also to two church communities for supporting me through my own dark places; believing in my journey even though it has often seemed fraught with pain and uncertainty. Christian Community Church stood with me as I began my own journey toward the contemplative tradition, and Barnabas Christian Fellowship has lived with me through nearly a decade of discovering ways of living the vision of love that we are coming to own.

I am also very grateful to the community of the Faithful Companions of Jesus here in Calgary who have opened their hearts to me so generously over the years. Sr. Nora Cummins became, in many ways, the midwife of my own recovery of love in God.

Finally, and most specially, I am grateful to my wife, Miriam, and my two daughters, Julie and Nikki, each in her own way so rich with the passion of life. I continually appreciate the honesty of love that we share in the community of our own family.

Reference Texts

The following books are used as the reference texts for the writings of the four authors introduced in this books. The quotations are used with permission from the publishers.

Edmund Colledge and James Walsh, trans. *Julian of Norwich: Showings.* New York: Paulist Press, 1978. The chapter notations for this source are from the Long Text.

James Wiseman, trans. *John Ruusbroec: The Spiritual Espousals and Other Works.* New York: Paulist Press, 1985. Notations by page number only.

Edmund Colledge, and Bernard McGinn, trans. *Meister Eckhart: The Essential Sermons, Commentaries, Treatises, Sermons and Defense.* New York: Paulist Press, 1981. Notations by German Sermon number.

Dorothy Sayers, trans. *The Comedy of Dante Alighieri: Hell.* Middlesex: Penguin Books, 1949. Notation by canto number.

————. *The Comedy of Dante Alighieri: Purgatory.* Middlesex: Penguin Books, 1955. Notation by canto number.

Dorothy Sayers and Barbara Reynolds, trans. *The Comedy of Dante Alighieri: Paradise.* Middlesex: Penguin Books, 1962. Notation by canto number.

Note on Inclusive Language

Many of the quotations cited in this book were written prior to the contemporary concern for inclusive language. While it has been impossible to modify the quotations themselves, the author has endeavored to use inclusive language in the body of the text. The author asks the reader to respond to the quotations with consideration for the context in which they were written.

PART I

The Meeting of Two Worlds

1

Our Contemporary Crisis of Intimacy

INTIMACY has become the great open wound in our culture. Nothing else compares to its pain or so strongly demands our attention.

We long to love and be loved, to be received somewhere, sometimes almost anywhere. We desperately want a place to rest.

Yet the mounting pain of broken relationships is erupting everywhere. Broken marriages, abuse and family violence, addictions, the isolation of single parents, the alienation from one's religious roots — these form a tragic litany of the wounds of intimacy. To those who must live with these wounds, who wonder if there will ever be an end to the pain, it may sound more like a broken record.

Each new experience of shattered dreams or broken relationship exposes the hurt and multiplies the longing. We do not live relatively stable lives with one or two sources of pain. What affects me most profoundly is the enormous pools of pain that people must contend with in almost every area of their lives.

Their family of origin has left them burdened with huge scars and open wounds. Their significant relationships are mired in cruelly dysfunctional behavior or teeter on the edge of collapse altogether. Their professions are not fulfilling and their attempts at leisure only heighten the pain of their normal existence. I wonder at times if I know anyone who has not personally been deeply affected by these hurts.

What are we struggling with and where is it going? Are we about the business of coping? For many, life is lived on such a thin edge that it is simply a matter of survival. There is little room or energy for any positive vision. Is that all that life has to offer any more?

The longing that emerges from these losses of love simply escalates until it becomes a sense of desperation. What are we to do with this growing passion?

Some try to suppress their longings as part of their dysfunctional behavior. It is their passion that has gotten them into this pain in the first place and so it must go.

Some try to manage their passion with better coping strategies. There is always another seminar to go to on how to live more effective lives.

Others have followed their desires by indulging passion with abandon. Yet consuming life has not brought the life it promised either. They have lived their passion until their lives have unraveled before their very eyes.

Where is the harmony, the integration? How can we find healing from our addictive and dysfunctional cycles? How can we recover from the wounds of love so that the passion can be savored and that love can be lived with freedom?

It is a haunting question. Neither the answer "stuff it" nor the answer "go with it" seem right. Neither the denial nor the indulgence of passion in themselves leads to healing.

Our world is in travail for love.

Perhaps this is just my own perspective, biased by my vocation. Do doctors wake up at night and conclude that the world is filled with hypochondriacs? How do dentists view the world at 2:00 a.m.?

I do not know. I do know that I hear a lot about people's longings and their pain in trying to find a positive experience of love. It is my job because I offer spiritual direction.

People tell me their stories. Each story is different, yet there is a common thread whether they come bursting with joy or bearing a tale of woe. Each person who comes to me wants to find the connections between his or her spiritual growth and everyday life.

The term "spiritual direction" has been brought back to popularity in the past few years. Admittedly, it has had its own checkered reputation in the past. Until recent years the term spiritual direction has conjured up for many Catholics images of a dour religious fanatic finding ways to make the directee's life painful and unenjoyable.

For many Protestants, the term is so new that it has little or no meaning. But in a search for a richer, more authentic spiritual experience, some are turning to spiritual direction with growing interest. Sometimes those with no Christian background understand the term as well as anyone.

Spiritual direction is the art of accompanying another in his or her spiritual growth. In Thomas Merton's words, "The whole purpose of spiritual direction is to penetrate beneath the surface of a man's life . . . to bring out his inner spiritual freedom."[3] Whatever may be the accepted meaning of the term, the essence of spiritual direction for me is to help people open up to the wonder of love. This exploration may be wide ranging. Personal significance, interpersonal relationships, learning to delight in the beauty of creation and finding a growing union with the Source of life that we call God — these are all part of the territory for exploration. They desire to find integrated lives, to learn to live in the world of love.

People who come for spiritual direction long to live, really live. They want to experience life openly and freely. The spiritual director's role is to encourage them to accept the life that is already there for them and to find their own "inner spiritual freedom."

My own work as a spiritual companion has been accented by people who struggle with their spirituality. Some are not sure they have a spiritual journey. Many have been deeply wounded in their religious past; others struggle with addictions or with the scars of abuse. Sometimes they come to me in the middle of marriage trauma, having lost all sense of their spiritual resources.

These people do not need another authority. They need to be encouraged to discover for themselves the unfolding of their own spiritual pilgrimage. They need permission. They want reassurance that their problems are not the demise of their spiritual life but the doorway to it.

Listening to people's stories has convinced me that whether they are beginning to ask deeper questions about their own spiritual growth, recovering from an addiction, struggling with an oppressive religious past, or working through some form of a dysfunctional relationship, all are in the business of seeking to recover a wholeness in love.

Coincidentally, my exploration of the mystical tradition within Christianity has convinced me that the great burden of the mystical writers centers on the mystery of love. They are mystical writers because they have pursued the mystery of love not because they are esoteric. Mysticism is simply the desire to experience union with all things and with God. These writers bring to us a vision of love that can validate our longing and help us find the way to that wholeness in love.

Returning to these writers in the history of Christian spirituality has increasingly convinced me that they have important things to say to us.

These writers understood that the longing for intimacy was deeper than a cultural problem. They knew that it is at the heart of our existence. They saw that the task of facing our wounds of intimacy and the compulsive and dependent ways we go about covering or compensating for those wounds is part of our positive growth toward love.

Further, they came to accept that this longing for intimacy, however gnarled and deformed and raw it might be, is a doorway to our destiny of union with our loving Creator. These themes are central to the whole Christian mystical tradition. However, I have chosen to limit our horizons to four fourteenth-century writers. There, in a chaotic and demoralizing social and religious milieu much like our own, they went to the heart of love and have left us a legacy of "communal memory" that we can no longer do without.

I trust that this book will bring the two streams of our present longing and of the mystical tradition into a fruitful union. If it is true that our addictive society is in travail for love, it is also true that there is a legacy within Christian mysticism that can help us on the road to recovery.

2

Religious Codependence

I T could well be that some of the most poignant losses of intimacy are found in religious experience. Spiritually too, many have lost the way of intimacy.

I am a pastor. I love Christianity. I am steeped in its images, but I am not blind to its pain. Those in recovery from addictive and codependent behavior frequently discover that their religious experience was part of their pain. It mirrored or reinforced what they experienced generally in their relationships.

In all honesty, it can be said that within the religious institution, "the household of faith," many were brought up in a dysfunctional family system.

These people can now look back and see that at the very place where they hoped for safety, a place of emotional acceptance and of loving exchange with God, they were often deprived of love and lived under the tyranny of fear.

Some people were literally abused. The power of the religious institution was so immersed in fear, so fear based, that it took advantage of their vulnerability. The cases of sexual abuse that have rocked the church establishment are not completely isolated events. They are the physical symptoms of a deeper violence.

Religious abuse carries with it the same traumatizing power of emotional and physical abuse. People come to me time and again deeply damaged because their experience of the religious system (which they identified with God) left them feeling intractably guilty and unlovable.

Many of us longed for love and were given expectations of religious duty. Like children bringing home our spiritual report cards, we could never do enough to find approval. The search for gentle, deep acceptance ended in fear, reprisal, and sometimes in violence.

Someone came to me a few weeks ago with this very paralyzing sense of God's anger and judgment. She grew up a good girl. She learned in Sunday School about God's love. She learned the little song that goes, "Be careful little eyes what you see...there's a Father up above and he's looking down in love, so be careful little eyes what you see" (adding a new part of the anatomy for each verse).

What a confusing and abusive contradiction in terms! Be careful, because God loves you.

What was the song supposed to be teaching? I had to ask the question myself because I was brought up with the same song. I do not know. But I do know what she learned. Whatever God's love was supposed to mean, for her it meant that she was to be afraid of everything she did because God could see everything and was going to punish her if she acted out of line.

Even those, like this woman, whose church tradition emphasized justification by faith and championed the notion of grace, found that their experience of spirituality was often shaped more by expectation, performance, and inadequacy than it was by acceptance, vitality, and possibility. Despite the doctrinal formulations which verbalized a concept of love, the value system that lay unverbalized underneath it all was one of fear which is the very antithesis of love.

Maybe some tried at times to risk passion, to cherish the vitality of life that they knew inside. Mostly, however, they were warned that passion is dangerous, that the world was dangerous and they must be always on guard.

So, like codependent children, they developed their own coping strategies and adopted roles in the religious family to live those strategies out.

Some became the superresponsible kid and did everything possible to keep the system intact. They were good. They defended the institution, exhausting themselves trying to support the very relationship that tyrannized them. Some of these people now come for spiritual direction, no longer knowing what spirituality is. They can no longer keep up the role of being responsible. Spiritual identity has been wrapped up in performance, but they are too tired to go on.

Others simply became the rebellious kid and positioned themselves against the family. They left religion with a horrible taste in their mouths, angry and bitter at the abuse they received.

Some, retreating like children into their rooms, slipped away into careers, leisure activities, or some other diversion. Once very active in various religious groups, they found that it was never enough. They could not live with the expectations on an ongoing basis. They could not always be "up" spiritually, and so they drifted to the sidelines. They would not risk again the wound of another attempt at intimacy in the family of God. Eventually they quietly accepted their role as spectators.

Do I say this to blame our religious past? No, surely not. The naming of our losses around intimacy and love in our religious experience is not to blame but to assess honestly our deficit balance. It gives us the impetus to choose for our own healing.

Blame does not take us anywhere. If anything has been discovered in the work of recovery, it is that blame does not solve our problems. No one grows up with intimacy and love perfectly provided and proportioned. The reality is that we are survivors not victims. We can now make choices toward our own healing.

If we grew up as religious codependents, and if we struggle with our blocks to intimacy, it is our privilege and responsibility to begin on the road to the recovery of love. There is healing for love and spirituality.

My Own Confession

What I really need to say is that I am describing my own journey. I am the one who knows so little about intimacy, the one who was "lost in my cortex" and was so emotionally disconnected that for years I did not recognize my own passion. I am the one who feels fractured in my society, who has struggled with my own forms of codependence and the ways my religious upbringing only reinforced those wounds of love. I am the one who, when anything goes wrong in the world, assumes that it must be my fault!

I can only trust that my experience is not unique. I see the wounds of intimacy in my world. And I talk to people every day who, in their deep pain, long to find a place where they can learn to grow in love.

3

Signs of the Recovery of Love

DESPITE the pain that marks our time and my own tendencies toward an "Eeyore" personality, I cannot help but be encouraged! The birth pangs may be terrible, but there might just be, imbedded in the pain, some very hopeful signs. Pointing to the wounds is not the whole story. Signs of energy give hope that the pain is not empty. These signs provide the impetus to keep moving toward the recovery of a healthy experience of intimacy and love.

Signs pointing to our recovery of love arise out of our own contemporary society. Learning to love and recovering the mystery of love has become one of the most significant tasks engaging our culture at present. This energy is not restricted to a few people. It is calling forth what appears to be another developmental stage in our entire society.

Children face a new primary task with each developmental stage of growth. So today, society is being called to face the loss of intimacy and to grow toward the possibility of loving as healthy people. Bringing love to birth is the unstated but very real end toward which a flood of cultural energy is being directed.

This burst of cultural energy expended in the recovery of love at present is focused especially in three important areas: the work being done in recovery from addictions and dysfunctional relationships; the growing hunger for spirituality and greater mystical consciousness; thirdly, the green movement to care for our planet.

These pains of labor promise the birth of something new. Each of these cultural movements points positively toward the recovery of love.

Addictions and Relational Recovery

The looming task of growth toward the recovery of love and intimacy energizes the phenomenal explosion of work in the area of recovery from addictions, from abuse, and from various forms of dysfunctional relationships.

Addictions are the ways people devise of medicating the pain of their deep wounds of intimacy. One becomes dependent on chemicals like alcohol or prescription drugs, on activities like work or sex, or on emotional patterns such as anger or depression. Clinging to these addictions masks the failures experienced in love and assuages, for a time, the enormous longing for love that threatens to overwhelm like a flood.

The very potency of the addictive qualities of these things points to the depth of our longing for love, of our pain, and of our need for some kind of euphoric or numbing substitute.

Dysfunctional relationships are only another form of addiction. They are desperate but distorted attempts to find intimacy at almost any price.

Children learn early in life how to get what they need and how to cope with the deprivations of love that they experience. While these coping mechanisms work successfully when we are younger, they become increasingly unsuccessful and finally destructive as we grow into adult life.

People live in abusive relationships and abuse others because they have lost love. They are angry and hurt and tormented. Gradually they learn to become dependent on others, manipulate others, and play any number of distorted games in order to secure some place to seek out a few morsels of love.

This is not just the "other people" — the prostitutes or the wife batterers. If we are honest, we can all tell our own story of distorted and destructive tendencies in our relationships.

But that is now changing. Many have tolerated the abuses and the twisted forms of intimacy long enough. They are recovering. Recovery is almost a magical word! It is charged with meaning around both the painful past and hopes and desires for the future.

Recovery is a bigger word than addiction or codependence. Words like addiction and codependence only remind us of our losses. They diagnose the ways we have learned to cope, medicate, or otherwise hide our wounds of love.

That naming process is good in itself. It can help pinpoint the direction for those who choose to work through the particular issues they are facing. Recovery, however, implies some sort of model of health. It poses a new question.

Why are we recovering? This focuses the real question. We have come to the place of choosing to break the cycle of destructive behavior. But to what end? Is it only to finally arrive in some tranquil, independent isolation?

Obviously, the whole aim of recovery is to enable a person to stand on his or her own two feet, to become an independently functional person. But the question still haunts us. Why become independently functional?

The only real answer to that question is that we want to reenter the incredible world of intimacy from a healthy place. Healing the wounds of love allows entry into love again, freely and truly.

We are, as it were, limping to the sidelines of the dance floor to recover. We have been trampled on in the dance. But we do not want to stay on the sidelines. We have just become aware of how wonderful the dance might be. Recovery is the process by which we can eventually get back into the beauty of the dance and enjoy the rest of the evening.

The Recent Explosion of Mysticism

The massive strength of the movement from dysfunctional relationships to a recovery of love is matched by an equally strong movement away from a sterile, fractured, rationally based world toward a world of interconnectedness, harmony, and heightened mystical consciousness.

A twentieth-century Christian mystic, Evelyn Underhill, defined mysticism as "the art of union with Reality."[4]

This simple definition encapsulates a major contemporary longing. Reality with a capital R implies the whole of life. People may no longer know how to define Reality, they may no longer accept traditional Christian definitions; yet they know there is more. That "more" has to do with the mystical union of all things.

If the whole of life is interconnected, then it is no longer satisfactory to be an observer tucked away in some safe, objective laboratory. People today want to participate. They want to be in the dance. They long for union.

Science, with its narrow dependence on rational analysis, is no longer the undisputed king of the castle. Like it or not, the bulk of our cultural energy has shifted from the university to health care. Rationality is not in dispute. But we have lived through a classic experience of addiction to rationality. The short term gain and long term destructive power of that addiction have become apparent.

What a breath of fresh air it has been to acknowledge that science does not hold all the keys to the world and that analytic, linear thought is not the only way to experience reality! People are discovering that they connect with their whole beings, bodies and all, to the whole of reality. This is a richness that seemed almost unimaginable a few years ago.

This radical shift toward wholeness, including spirituality, was not simply a revolt against the tyranny of idolizing rational, linear thought. It has also been a much needed reaction to the horror of personal and social disintegration.

Western society has analyzed itself and its world into tiny fragments. Like little children, we learned how to take things apart, but in the process we forgot how things went together. We have been taught to analyze, classify, and name, but have lost the wonder of union with the whole.

Life has been compartmentalized and fragmented until our very existence on this planet is threatened. As long as life was atomized, ecology did not matter.

Many now are seeking spirituality. They are running toward union. They want to find themselves in the All, to rediscover intimacy with the whole of existence.

Christians, many from the more conservative denominations,

are asking questions about spirituality and the mystical tradition. Many have found the spirituality expressed by their tradition out of touch with their experience. They long for an authentic personal experience of their faith. One of the places they are turning for spiritual nourishment is to the great spiritual writers in Christian history.

These writers speak to the longing people experience for union, to their desire to integrate their faith with the whole of reality.

It is a healthy sign. People are no longer quite so concerned about getting it right; they want to get it real.

It is no accident that we are seeking recovery from addictions and seeking a greater mystical union at the same time. Like the work in recovery, the work in expanding consciousness is also a cry for intimacy, for union. It is a longing to recover love.

Ironically, this attraction to a more mystical spirituality is often regarded as dangerous or is simply repudiated by the Church. The new spiritual sensibility does not necessarily respond to traditional religious vocabulary. Further, it is decidedly anti-institutional in its outcry against religious oppression. The waters have been muddied.

In an age of empiricism, the church held sway in the realm of metaphysics, if anyone cared to listen. Now the field has been swamped with new voices, each claiming spiritual awareness. One should not be overly surprised at the careful and sometimes defensive response by the church.

The new mysticism, including the New Age movement, is certainly not an unqualified good. It is ravenous like a great white shark, feeding on almost anything. And while that image may not say much for discretion within the movement, it does indicate its appetite. People are starving for love.

The Concern for a Green Planet

A third and very hopeful evidence of our desire to recover love is the explosion of environmental consciousness. In 1980 only a few dedicated countercultural types celebrated Earth Day. In 1990 millions of people around the world gathered to promote the care of our planet.

The green movement is part of our longing to find union. Realization has dawned (even admittedly out of self-interest for survival) that they cannot live in isolation from nature anymore. Nature can no longer be treated as something to be exploited. We are coming to the awareness that the only way to preserve the fragile world in which we live is to come *to love it*. We are slowly seeing the wisdom of the Native Americans who lived in a relationship of communion with the world around them.

All three of these movements predominate the landscape of our contemporary consciousness. The massive energy being poured into recovery, into a heightened mystical consciousness, and into the preservation of our natural home points to the reality that we in our society are looking for more. All three movements indicate that the "more" we are searching for has to do with connectedness, with intimacy, with a vision of love.

There is another cluster of signs, this time from our past, that offers us hope. It reminds one of an old heirloom just being uncovered after years of being in the attic. Six hundred years ago, in an equally chaotic century, four people independently faced their own longings for love. Their legacy to us, some of the great mystical writings of the Christian tradition, provides confirmation and inspiration as we face our own struggle to learn to love freely and passionately.

4

Our Mirrored Selves

FOURTEENTH-CENTURY Europe seems such an unlikely place to find a vision for our day, and such an unlikely time. Could it really be that, as the medieval period drew to a close, voices were raised (and for centuries almost lost) that help us rediscover our vision of love?

Yet in the writings of Julian of Norwich, John Ruusbroec, Meister Eckhart, and Dante Alighieri is found the greatest exploration of love ever produced.

It is more common to think of the medieval period as the source of many religious woes. Wasn't it then, when religion ruled supreme, that so many of our distortions of spirituality emerged?

Wasn't it then, when the church was so powerful, that the corruption of power produced a religion of fear and guilt from which we are still reeling in the twentieth century? Isn't it from just such a religious mentality that, in Vatican II and parallel movements in other church traditions, we are finally beginning to escape?

Yes, there were abuses. It was the breaking up of a long hegemony of religious rule. But now as we are approaching the end of the hegemony of the age of reason, we can better see how the stereotypes and biases of rationalism focused on the abuses and kept us from the wealth of that tumultuous century. We are finally

35

in a better place to see what is offered for us without having to cast the message in terms of fear and guilt.

The title and subtitle of Barbara Tuchman's history of the period, *A Distant Mirror: The Calamitous Fourteenth Century,*[5] draw a graphic picture of the relationship between the fourteenth century and our time. She well knows that there are differences but beyond the differences there are fundamental similarities to our own apocalyptic era. Perhaps the circumstances of that long-ago time will resonate with the themes of your own present experience.

Most dramatically, and easily recognizable, the fourteenth century was a time of colossal catastrophe. In our own century two world wars, the demoralizing reality of the holocaust, the threat of nuclear disaster, the spectre of AIDS, and the horror of global hunger have forever altered our perception of life.

The fourteenth century suffered some of the same sort of apocalyptic events. The black plague ravaged Europe, killing an estimated one third of the population living between India and Iceland. In Norwich alone, where Julian lived through all three outbreaks, over half the clergy was wiped out by the disease. This was disaster on an unprecedented scale. Nothing of the kind had ever been known to happen before. Death was everywhere; it touched every family. The dead were taken out by cartloads every day, and still it was impossible to keep up with the grisly advance of the disease.

If the holocaust has challenged our views of the justice of God or even of God's existence, what must the black plague have meant to that century. In some measure at least, the holocaust can be seen as the outbreak of human evil. People chose to perpetrate the holocaust. The black plague could not be blamed on the perversity of human will. It was a travesty of nature from which no one completely escaped.

The chaotic effects of the black plague were as devastating as the plague itself. Spiritually, psychologically, and emotionally the world completely changed. The old security of cosmic unity collapsed and the new had to be rebuilt along some other lines. Fear was rampant and escape from fear into many different kinds of refuge, including wild religious ecstasy, was everywhere.

Secondly, the century was a time of economic collapse and of political instability. The feudal system was breaking down under growing nationalism and the rise of the mercantile system. What people had come to accept as normal was suddenly being challenged all around them.

Along with this, early in the century, there was severe crop failure and the onslaught of famine. In England, particularly, this economic failure was heightened by the fact that the fourteenth century was also the century of the Hundred Years' War with France. That war completely drained the economic resources of both countries.

With the political and economic changes came a whole new series of questions. What was the place of the common person? Were the poor allowed to challenge the system in order to benefit their own lot in life? Was it selfish and out of place to demand reforms? Was it healthy despite the fact that it created conflict? These kinds of questions lay just below the surface of the political and economic changes.

The entire political and social order that had been reinforced by the religious institutions was now in transition. Was it a betrayal of one's religion to call for change? Here the questions of survival in the culture and spirituality met head on.

Although the particular examples have changed, many of the same questions are being faced today. The changes in what is considered normal end up challenging our concept of what spirituality and religious convictions are all about.

The third parallel to our own time, perhaps less dramatic but more powerful, was the breakup of medieval culture as a unified system of belief and behavior. Seeds of awareness that had been sown over a period of time came to fruition. Combined with revolutionary changes in the political and economic structures of Europe, these seeds became the basis of a new, emerging way of perceiving the world. What we now call the Renaissance was well on its way to toppling the unified structure of the medieval world view.

This shift from the medieval world view to a new way of perceiving reality is important for us to consider. It was a time of transition from religion to science. It was a shift away from a unified world view in which everything was interconnected and eventually linked to a cosmic Center. In the medieval world all things had spiritual significance.[6]

We know of that in its worst forms, of course, because the rationalistic tradition in which we were raised made sure we saw its perversions. In its worst forms the sensual and the human were reduced to being incidental. People and things existed only for the sake of their spiritual significance and not for the significance they might bear in their own right.

The movement away from a unified universe was also a movement toward a world where humanity was liberated from an oppressive hierarchy of spiritual significance to an independent existence.

With the center of the universe shifted from the One to the particulars, from the Divine to the human, reason became the dominant means of perceiving the world. Reason was especially adapted to figure out the world in terms of its parts without reference to its connections. Humanity was becoming the center of the universe and human rationality the judge of all things. It was the dawning of the age of the Enlightenment.

Finally, the fourteenth century was a time of unprecedented religious upheaval. Both theologically and morally the church was in a time of chaos.

New ways of seeing the world challenged the church and its theology. At the close of the thirteenth century Thomas Aquinas synthesized an entirely new theological system. He changed the way theology was conceived by using the newly recovered philosophical notions of Aristotle as they were brought to the West by Averroes, a Muslim.[7]

That sounds so natural for us today. But all we have to do is look at our own concerns about theology and consider the impact of someone restructuring the whole framework by borrowing from contemporary "infidels," and we can begin to feel the uncertainty and fear that was present as the fourteenth century opened.

Along with the theological confusion there was a deep sense of alienation because of religious corruption. Priests and bishops openly flaunted the children produced from their various sexual liaisons. Perhaps if lived as a protest to clerical celibacy, that might not have been so bad, but it was lived while espousing the virtue of celibacy as the official position of the church.

Worse still, for much of the fourteenth century there were two and even three popes grasping for power. The Great Schism and the so-called Babylonian Captivity of the church was the dominant reality in the institutional church of the fourteenth century.

In sum, the fourteenth century was not what we might call a nurturing religious climate for producing a vision of love filled with such power that it still holds value for us today! Yet in this chaos, and perhaps because of it, some in that century explored the far reaches of love. It is to them that we will go to rediscover our "communal memory."

Looking back from our own century, the crises of the fourteenth century give us a sense of partnership. These writers faced a world like ours. They did not speak from a happy, well-ordered world and pronounce pious directives about how we should get our lives together and control our passion.

Those who desire to deepen their spirituality, whether Christian or not, will find that these writers point the way to the recovery of love.

PART II

Julian of Norwich

The Environment of Love
and the
Healing of Trust

Limitless love,
from the depths to the stars:
   flooding all,
   loving all.
It is the royal kiss of peace.

>   —Hildegard of Bingen[8]

You speak of my beginnings?
I will tell you.

> I was created in love

> For that reason
> Nothing can express my beauty
>   nor liberate my nobleness
> Except love alone.

>   —Mechtild of Magdeburg[9]

5

Is the Universe a Friendly Place?

WHEN asked, "What is the most important question a person can ask?" Albert Einstein is said to have replied, "Is the universe a friendly place or not?"[10]

In the present transition from the old era to an uncertain future, the question becomes monumental. Even more than the fourteenth century, our time is crammed to overflowing with change.

It was Percy Bysshe Shelley who looked at his nineteenth century world (which we would now call relatively stable) and wrote a poem entitled "Mutability." Change, says Shelley, is the only unchangeable thing we have.

> We are as clouds that veil the midnight moon;
>> How restlessly they speed, and gleam, and quiver,
> Streaking the darkness radiantly! — yet soon
>> Night closes round, and they are lost forever: . . .
>
> Man's yesterday may ne'er be like his morrow;
>> Nought may endure but Mutability.[11]

What would he have said in the last decade of the twentieth century when even the syndrome of change trauma known as future shock is now old news and forgotten?

Each new day brings a new disintegration of what we have held to be normal. This loss of a sense of normal is terribly threatening. Einstein's question burrows into our hears and eats away at our confidence to trust love.

What does a normal family look like anymore? What is a normal marriage? What constitutes a normal career, normal friendship, normal sexual expression, normal political expectation, normal experience of church?

Is the universe a friendly place? Just posing the question terrorizes us.

If it were only the shock of change that threatened us, we might cope. But our children are growing up in increasingly violent family and social systems. If change threatens trust, violence provokes paralysis.

It is estimated that one in every three women have been sexually abused. Children who live as victims of violence come to believe in a violent universe. Violence is normal. They grow up with a deeply ingrained fear of the world and a crippling inability to be vulnerable enough to open up to love again. How are they to answer Einstein's question?

Is their essential posture in the world one of confidence or one of encroaching terror?

Many dysfunctional coping strategies are nothing more than fortifications against a hostile universe. Love cannot blossom and intimacy is impossible if we remain closed off in walls of distrust and fear. We cannot open up to life if we have learned to disconnect from life to cope with abuse.

Fear dominates and controls how people live in the marketplace, how they live in their marriages and friendships, in the parenting of their children, and in the way they face old age.[12]

Trembling with emotion, someone said to me last week, "Even my church is no longer a safe place." And in that one sentence he summed up a whole lifetime of fear — running from family conflict, child abuse, fear of rejection from his wife, and now even the place of faith and trust was a place of change and terror.

If life is going by too fast, if we can't respond quickly enough to get it right, if the Source of life is an unhappy Judge, what hope is there that we might recover love?

Are we safe here? I know of no other question that names so

much of what many experience in trying to find a place to stand in our world today.

As we seek to recover our vision of love, the question is crucial. If we are to risk living passionately, we must have some confidence that we will be received. If there is going to be any opening up to love there must be reassurance that love will be there for us, that we are held in love. We must find a way to trust.

A hermit in Norwich, England, looked through her window at the devastation of her century and gently reassured those who came to her for help that life is good, that we are created in love and for love.

Julian of Norwich anticipated the question asked by Einstein by six centuries! She did not see, in the evil of her day, a final indictment of life. Nor did she see in the suffering of Jesus, the face of the cosmic Judge. She saw the smile of Love.

Julian's great gift is to reveal the love that undergirds all things and permeates the entire environment of our lives. To rest in this love as the central fact of the universe is to heal the wounds of trust and enable us to risk love again.

6

Julian's Own Experience

THE Revelations of Divine Love[13] is Mother Julian's great legacy to the world. Love permeates her writing just as she saw it permeating creation. Her book becomes a picture of the universe she describes. And when we have finished reading what she wrote, we find, if we have listened at all, that love has begun to permeate us as well.

In our jaded and cynical time we are easily tempted to dismiss her as a sentimental ecstatic, a religious Harlequin romance. How can anyone who faces into the global suffering today talk any longer about a good universe and the idea that we are created and sustained in love?

Maybe that was good enough for naive nineteenth-century optimism, but postholocaust theology faces the serious question of whether there is a God at all, let alone a good God who suffuses life with love.

This question is fair and a cynical conclusion is entirely possible. But then, another question echoes back, how could Julian be so optimistic when she lived through the events of the fourteenth century? Can she be so easily dismissed?

Born in late 1342, the woman we know by the name Julian lived most of her life cloistered in a cell attached to the church

46

of St. Julian in Norwich and was devoted to prayer and informal spiritual direction.

Julian (almost certainly not her real name) gives us very little personal information. What we do know from surrounding history is that Julian lived through the three great outbreaks of the black plague. And during her lifetime England and France wore themselves out in the Hundred Years' War.

Ravaged by the plague, food shortage, and the war, England was bankrupt. Someone had to pay. The nobility, reluctant to reduce their extravagant lifestyle, saddled the already oppressed peasants with the burden. An oppressive poll tax was levied in 1380 and the peasants finally revolted.

Julian could not help but be aware of the peasants' anguish and of the part her own bishop, the bishop of Norwich, played in the cruel suppression of the uprising.

The peasants were not the only ones to feel the bishop's iron handshake. A lay reform movement in the church in England was growing under the leadership of John Wyclif and his followers, the Lollards.

The suppression of the reform movement grew in intensity until it, too, became violent. Within a few years of Julian's life, many of these reformers were put to death in what became known as the Lollard pit. The Lollard pit was located just outside Norwich.

Significant as each of these events was, none is mentioned directly by Julian. She could not have been ignorant of them, but she does not discuss them. They merely form the backdrop of her own deepening movement into God.

She does not spend time analyzing the events of her world. She goes behind them, forced perhaps behind them by the very events themselves, to see if there is any substance to life as we know it.

Julian's method reveals something as important to us as the content of what she has to say. It is necessary to ask the hard questions in the light of the events of this century and our own personal experience. Given the horrible experiences of abuse that people have suffered, they cannot but face the very real question that the universe is hostile. Love seems like a bad joke and trust seems naive.

But the movement toward cynicism and despair is not life-giving. It does not open up to choices. If we see only the great evil of these events, we will begin to see ourselves as victims and lose any sense of our own possibility.

Somewhere we have to find a place to nurture life and hope. We have to find a ground on which we can begin to trust again. It is the possibility that love is the center of life, more fundamental than the deepest evil, that brings hope and the power of choice to us in our present life experience.

From her own writing we do know that at the age of thirty she received a series of visions of Jesus on the cross. Along with these visions, Julian became sick and almost died.

Those experiences became pivotal in her life, and she spent the next twenty years praying through the implications of what she had experienced. The fruit of that long process of listening, picturing, reasoning, and responding is the book we now call *The Revelations of Divine Love* or the *Showings*.

Julian's reflections are characterized by maturity, boldness, and wisdom. She expressly states that she allowed the reality of her own unique experience, the exercise of her "kyndly" (natural) reason, the teaching of the church, and the inner promptings of the Spirit to inform and shape her conclusions. The result is an integration of unsurpassed power and beauty. Thomas Merton wrote that Julian of Norwich

> is without doubt one of the most wonderful of all Christian voices. She gets greater and greater in my eyes as I grow older, and whereas in the old days I used to be crazy for St John of the Cross, I would not exchange him now for Julian if you gave me the world and the Indies and all the Spanish mystics rolled up in one bundle. I think that Julian of Norwich is with Newman the greatest English theologian.[14]

7

The Heartbeat of the Universe

COMING to the text of the *Showings* will provide a glimpse into the depth of Julian's insight. We will see that Julian places us in a universe encompassed in love. Then we will hear her discuss how the revelations she received helped her to perceive our essential dignity. Julian says that we are one with God at the essence of who we are. Finally, we will see the pictures that Julian gives to show us the loving care with which we are held even at the places of pain and brokenness.

Love: The Heartbeat of the Universe

When we turn from the twentieth century to read Julian, we are dismayed to discover, at the outset, pages of graphic, almost grue-some descriptions of the physical suffering and bleeding of Jesus. She writes,

> At this I saw the red blood running down from under the crown, hot and flowing freely and copiously. (chap. 4)

> The hot, red blood ran out so plentifully that neither skin nor wounds could be seen, but everything seemed to be blood. (chap. 12)

49

After this Christ showed me part of his Passion, close to his death. I saw his sweet face as it were dry and bloodless with the pallor of dying, and then deadly pale, languishing, and then the pallor turning blue and then the blue turning brown, as death took more hold upon his flesh. (chap. 26)

It sounds melodramatic and excessively morbid to our sophisticated ears. Frankly, it has been enough to keep many contemporary readers from reading further.

In Julian's day, Franciscan spirituality was very popular in England. A great deal of devotion focused on the physical sufferings of Jesus. Julian's own perceptions were no different. The bodily suffering of Jesus is the starting point of her spirituality.

When we take a second look, however, we discover that, despite the graphic descriptions, Julian did not emphasize the suffering of Jesus but the revelation of love seen in the suffering.

Her descriptions of Jesus' suffering are not given to evoke our sense of guilt. Jesus' passion has so often been linked with sinfulness and guilt that to hear once more that Jesus suffered for us only reinforces our already crippled sense of spiritual self worth.

For Julian, the crucifixion was the doorway to love, not to morbidity or blame. She opens her book with these words,

Here begins the first chapter. This is the revelation of *love* which Jesus Christ, our endless bliss, made in sixteen showings. (chap. 1)

And then after more than eighty chapters describing and meditating on the showings she concludes with a remarkable statement which encapsulates her whole book. She writes that she heard the words,

What, do you wish to know your Lord's meaning in this thing? Know it well, love was his meaning. Who reveals it to you? Love. Why does he reveal it to you? For love. Remain in this, and you will know more of the same. But you will never know different, without end. (chap. 86)

For her, the love of God displayed in the suffering of Jesus is the final demonstration that our world, despite its pain, and in the midst of its pain, is deeply loved. Her first and deepest awareness was not the convulsions of pain which racked her world, but the passionate love in which her fragile universe was held.

So Julian rushes from the introductory material of the first four chapters to begin unfolding the content and implications of her vision. Immediately she is caught up in love.

> At the same time as I saw this sight of the head bleeding, our good Lord showed a spiritual sight of his familiar love. I saw that he is to us everything which is good and comforting for our help. He is our clothing, who wraps and enfolds us for love, embraces us and shelters us, surrounds us for love, which is so tender that he may never leave us. (chap. 5)

This is the essence, the heart and core of her understanding of life. We are clothed with, wrapped in and enfolded for love. Nothing could be more permeating, more total and more overwhelming. It is the theme she will elucidate and illustrate in innumerable ways in the book.

She then specifies what she means by being clothed and enfolded for love. She began to see an image of something small in her hand, no bigger than a hazelnut. As she contemplated this she was amazed at its ongoing existence. It seemed that it should disintegrate.

Here is one of those hints that Julian understood the chaos of her century. Life should not hold together. Life as we know it seems too small, too fragile to survive if the universe is as hostile as it seems.

Put in contemporary terms, survivors of abuse and addictive patterns begin to wonder if there can be any future after the pain. Is not the pain too overwhelming? Will the pain ever end, and if it does, will there be anything left with which to begin building life again?

But Julian is surprised. Life does survive, even through the black plague. Then she says she was answered in her understanding,

> It lasts and always will last because God loves it; and thus everything has being through the love of God. In this little thing I saw three properties. The first is that God made it, the second is that God loves it, and the third is that God preserves it. (chap. 5)

Evelyn Underhill uncovers some of the depth of this passage in her words,

> This whole changeful natural order, with all its apparent collisions, cruelties, and waste, yet springs from an ardour, an immeasurable love, a perpetual donation, which generates it, upholds it, drives it; for "all-thing hath being by the love of God" ... everything says Julian in effect, whether gracious, terrible, or malignant, is enwrapped in love; and is part of a world produced, not by mechanical necessity, but by passionate desire.[15]

Love is not simply the benevolent act of God in providing a nice place to live or that rescues us from the bad world. Love is the heartbeat of the universe.

Love is the very soul of life, of all springing up, of all mating and union and of all fruition. The universe is not made with mechanical necessity. Economic efficiency is not the bottom line. It is conceived and born and suffused with passionate desire.

Life, burgeoning and blooming, the promise of birth and the tenacity of weeds growing between the cracks in the sidewalks are all manifestations of passionate love. To be alive, to choose to open up to life, is to participate in the love that flows in the veins of our existence.

This desire that surrounds us and inflames us is the presence of God who loves the world into being and sustains it with that same passion of love. It is no wonder then that Julian can end this chapter with the startling words,

> Our good Lord revealed that it is very greatly pleasing to him that a simple soul should come naked, openly and familiarly. For this is the loving yearning of the soul through the touch of the Holy Spirit. (chap. 5)

It is almost too much for restless, heartbroken twentieth-century-weary people to hear. Our deepest yearning is to be able to approach the heart of the universe openly and without fear. We want to belong, to be safe. We long to find a place where we can be naked and open and familiar (Julian's term for intimate).

Julian bids us to stop hiding and come openly to God. We do not need to deny our fear, but gently we can begin to move from fear to trust. We can come nakedly because we will be received. We can risk living because life finds its source in the love of God.

8

Discovering Our Deepest Truth

IT is not easy for me to write about learning to trust love. It has been one of the hardest things for me to come to accept in my own spiritual pilgrimage. My personal journal reflects the deep sense of abandonment I struggle with inside.

> I do not start with the truth [of abandonment] to be proved but with the feeling always already present, needing only to be corroborated by some experience of negation or some refusal of what I had hoped for.

> I am predisposed to abandonment. It has colored all I do and how I think. I am afraid to trust people, afraid to evoke their anger. I am afraid to try and fail, afraid to try and succeed.

> Life begins with emptiness and is never finally filled. I hobble into life already maimed, waiting for disaster to fall, for my favorite things to be yanked away like dangerous toys.

Staying with Julian has challenged that predisposition to abandonment with a deeper, truer perception. I am gradually coming to the conclusion, emotionally and not just intellectually, that the deepest truth within me is that I enter life with my world of abandonment already held in love.

54

I can hear my own inner critic reply, "It is not good enough to be a bad person in a good universe. It is no help to see the world as loved into being by God if I still see myself as broken and alien." If that sounds trivial, let me illustrate.

Rightly or wrongly, I grew up associating the communion service with the crucifixion. In that solemn service we were to picture our unworthiness before God through meditating on the Christ's sufferings in his broken body and shed blood as symbolized by the communion emblems. Awareness of our unworthiness and Christ's sufferings was to motivate us to live in greater obedience.

Somehow, it seemed to me, God was making me an offer I couldn't refuse. It made love seem oppressive and abusive, an obligation to receive and a duty to perform.

We would not tolerate that kind of behavior on the part of a parent toward a child. Imagine the scars of a child growing up believing that his father was basically angry with him. In his anger the father threatens to run over the child with his car. At the last moment the father stops the car. He gets out, hovers over the child and says, "I could have run over you, but out of love I stopped the car. You better keep that solemn fact in mind from now on and be careful to obey me."

That may sound ridiculous, even blasphemous. I do not suggest this was how people in my tradition saw God, but it is the way I ended up perceiving who God was. It is not the true picture of God nor of the suffering of Jesus. But it is the deep, sometimes unarticulated view many people have of God. It becomes a very manipulative and abusive experience of love.

I can picture coming to Julian's cell in Norwich. She might lean out her window a little more than usual to whisper, "Love is the beginning and the end. God our Mother wants us to be very safe. Just climb up into her lap and let her kiss you better!"

Julian's theology is deeper than sin and judgment. Her incentive for love is deeper than fear. She does not deny sin, she sees that in Jesus sin has been superseded. We can come to God without fear because love bids us welcome. John the Apostle spoke of the healing of trust when he said, "There is no fear in love. But perfect love drives out fear, because fear has to do with punishment ... we love because he first loved us" (1 John 4:18, 19a).

Julian's conviction that God holds the entire universe in tender love is made specific by the ways she describes who God is and who we are. God holds a fragile universe in love. God loves us in our goodness and in our poverty and brokenness.

Julian's Images of God

God not only creates and sustains the universe in love, God also is fully open to us in love.

We can examine only a tiny portion of Julian's images of God. Two particular images of God invite us into a relationship of love, especially when we are broken by our failed attempts to love and be loved.

First, Julian describes God as a nobleman who chooses to become intimate with a peasant. Given the circumstances surrounding the peasants' revolt in Julian's own time, it is not a pious, paternalistic image. It is a revolutionary image of social justice.

> He showed me this plain example. It is the greatest honour which a majestic king or a great lord can do for a poor servant, to be familiar with him; and especially if he makes this known himself, privately and publicly, with great sincerity and happy mien, this poor creature will think: See, what greater honour and joy could this noble lord give me than to demonstrate to me who am so little, this wonderful familiarity? Truly, this is a greater joy and delight to me than if he were to give me great gifts, and himself always to remain distant in his manner. (chap. 7)

Julian pushes this image one step further. Not only is the nobleman on intimate terms with the peasant, she sees the nobleman at home in his great palace, our soul (her term for the center of our being).

> And then our good Lord opened my spiritual eye, and showed me my soul in the midst of my heart. I saw the soul as wide as if it were an endless citadel, and also as if it were a blessed kingdom, and from the state which I saw in it, I understood that it is a fine city. In the midst of that city sits our Lord Jesus,

true God and true man, a handsome person and tall, highest bishop, most awesome king, most honourable lord. (chap. 68)

That honourable city in which our Lord Jesus sits is our sensuality, in which he is enclosed; and our natural substance is enclosed in Jesus. (chap. 56)

The place chosen to be the royal palace must be the most beautiful place. So, Julian concludes, a person's inner being must be the most beautiful part of creation.

The second image that Julian gives of God has become famous in our day. As a fourteenth century woman she speaks openly of God as Mother.

From this it follows that as truly as God is our Father, so truly is God our Mother. (chap. 58)

And so I saw that God rejoices that he is our Father, and God rejoices that he is our Mother. (chap. 52)

As our Mother, God is the womb of our being, the breast of our nurture, and the lap to which we can run when we get into trouble or hurt ourselves.

But often when our falling and our wretchedness are shown to us, we are so much afraid and so greatly ashamed of ourselves that we scarcely know where we can put ourselves. But then our courteous Mother does not wish us to flee away, for nothing would be less pleasing to him; but he then wants us to behave like a child. For when it is distressed or frightened, it runs quickly to its mother; and when it can do no more, it calls to the mother for help with all its might. (chap. 62)

Julian deliberately chooses images of God that demonstrate God's undeterred love for us. It does not have anything to do with our achievement or status. It is one thing to feel loved by God when one's life is together. One can feel strong when all the normal support systems are in place. At least the facade of health can be maintained. But what happens when life falls through the cracks, and all the natural images of love seem distant and even hostile?

Ask anyone who has just gone through a separation or divorce. Are they now a whole being? Do they have worth? Are they still lovable, especially by God? Julian's image of God as a Mother heightens the awareness that God is there to love us not to judge us.

Julian's Images of Human Beings

Creation is alive with the love of God. God is always there for us in love. There is more, Julian maintains. We too, as people, are grounded in God in our essential being. We "dwell" in God and God dwells in us.

We do not really know who we are, claims Julian. Caught up in the chaos of our external circumstances, we have lost sight of our true selves. She says, "Our passing life which we have here does not know in our senses what our self is" (chap. 46).

Who then are we? Julian responds with a deeply affirming description of our being. Human beings are not divided by body and soul as in the familiar categories of material and spiritual. Julian, following Aquinas, speaks of our being as substantial and sensual.

These words are used differently today. Substance, today, has the connotation of physically solid; sensual often carries sexual overtones. Julian uses the term substance to describe the essence, the center of one's being. It does mean solid, the solid core of who we are. Sensuality, for Julian, meant any part of a person that was changeable, that interacted with and was affected by the external world.

Our sensuality, according to Julian, is our aware self. Our sensuality would include our intellect, our feelings and our self-concept. Our sensuality is that part of us open to the world around us, our substance is our deepest, unchanging self.

The core of our being, our substance, always was, is, and always shall be united with God in love.

> God is essence in his very nature. . . . He is the ground, his is the substance, and he is the true Father and true Mother of natures. (chap. 62)

Our sensuality, the part affected by our world, is changeable and can experience brokenness and pain.

> Greatly ought we to rejoice that God dwells in our soul; and more greatly ought we to rejoice that our soul dwells

in God. Our soul is created to be God's dwelling place, and the dwelling of our soul is God, who is uncreated. It is a great understanding to see and know inwardly that God, who is our Creator, dwells in our soul, and it is a far greater understanding to see and know inwardly that our soul, which is created, dwells in God in substance, of which substance, through God, we are what we are.

And I saw no difference between God and our substance, but, as it were, all God, and still my understanding accepted that our substance is in God, that is to say that God is God, and our substance is a creature in God. (chap. 54)

This is the starting point of our being. It is the first truth about us. We are encompassed in God and rooted in God. We are made in the image of God as the biblical writers express it.

Julian's description of personal significance does not deny our failings, nor the need for help. But it describes what is true of us before sin and deeper than sin. For Julian, redemption is our being "oned" with God in grace in our external selves as we already are in nature. It is coming home not only to God but also to our true selves.[16]

Recovery is, in a real sense, the recovery of our essential self. This is the message that Meister Eckhart will confirm so strongly.

9

Love and Our Wounds

WE are enfolded for love by a loving, intimate God who lives in us and we in God. That starting point has monumental implications for our unfolding spirituality.

Julian emphasizes two of those implications in her discussion of sin and her view of prayer.

Sin and Love

The way Julian deals with sin helps us see how often we have begun at the wrong starting point: we have emphasized sin, egocentricity, and the need for healing.

While Julian never denies that those things are true of us, she refuses to see them as primary. She says that our goodness is deeper than our brokenness. Our very being is in God. Our substance is found in God and God in us.

> God judges us in our natural substance, which is always kept one in him, whole and safe, without end ... man judges us in our changeable sensuality, which now seems one thing and now another, as it derives from parts and presents an external appearance. (chap. 45)

This is the first and primary truth about us. She then concludes that if our being is grounded in God and in love, the primary motivation of our heart is toward union with God. "Our natural will is to have God and God's natural will is to have us" (chap. 6). Humanity is created in love and its basic desire is to return to the love of its Creator.

Sin is secondary. It exists but is not "substantial." It is painful, but it will not destroy the work of God. The wounds we experience in life are doorways to that journey back into God.

Julian is startling in her discussion of sin. She begins by anticipating the questions one might have in the face of such a positive view of the universe, of God, and of humanity. We might sigh a little wistfully and say, "Isn't it beautiful. Too bad it isn't true! If only there was no sin or evil we could believe in this kind of world."

Julian herself says,

And after this our Lord brought to my mind the longing that I had for him before, and I say that nothing hindered me but sin, and I saw that this is true of us all in general, and it seemed to be that if there had been no sin, we should all have been pure and as like our Lord as he created us. (chap. 27)

The response that is given to her are these famous lines,

Sin is necessary, but all will be well, and all will be well, and every kind of thing will be well. (chap. 27)

Is it religious idealism, ostrichlike naivete? She struggles with the response herself. But without trying to solve the question of the origin of evil, she does give us a place to stand in relation to sin in holding a positive vision of love.

First of all, she declares that sin is a secondary fact. In describing her vision of the ugly suffering of Jesus she says,

But I did not see sin, for I believe that it has no kind of substance, no share in being, nor can it be recognized except by the pain caused by it. (chap. 27)

From there she goes on to state the worst case scenario. She declares (much like St. Paul's own statements of the triumph of grace), "I shall do nothing at all but sin; and my sin will not impede the operation of his goodness" (chap. 36). If sin is secondary, then sin will not overcome the basic intent of God to work goodness. If sin has no substance then I can rest assured that my "screw ups" in life, as bad as they are, will not wreck the whole program. Whether or not I measure up will not stop God's loving work in my life.

Instead, she says that although she began to fear when she thought about her sin she was reassured by love, "And in this I conceived a gentle fear, and in answer to this our Lord said: I protect you very safely" (chap. 37).

Finally, she boldly states that "sin will be no shame, but honor" (chap. 38). Then for the rest of the chapter she reminds the reader of examples from the Old Testament like David, from the New Testament like Mary Magdalene and Peter, and from her own contemporary experience (St. John of Beverly). These all had their share of failure and pain, yet their stories only become part of a greater story. They are remembered with honor for the ways in which God worked goodness through the pain of their own experience.

Sin, then, is not to be the focus of our attention. We need not be consumed with an image of failure and guilt.

It is not that Julian ignores sin. She merely chooses to give it the consideration it deserves, second place! Then she turns right around and says that these places of failure and pain are the means by which we are opened up to God. "Sin," she says, "is the sharpest scourge with which any chosen soul can be struck" (chap. 39).

Failure opens us up to honesty and then to the loving care of God. It is through facing up to our failures in an atmosphere of love that we are healed. But she reminds us again that "our courteous Lord does not want his servants to despair because they fall often and grievously; for our falling does not hinder him in loving us" (chap. 39).

Prayer and Love

Finally, to be grounded in love means that our deepest desire is to experience union with God, and that desire is our prayer. Julian's discussion of prayer is focused on this truth.

Prayer is essentially the expression of our heart longing for love.

It is not so much the listing of our requests but the breathing of our one deepest request, to be united with God as fully as possible.

We are often unsure whether God hears us because we feel unworthy and because we "are not feeling anything at all; for often we are as barren and dry after our prayers as before" (chap. 41).

Her reply is that God is the ground of our prayer. Where does the longing for union come from anyway? What is the source of our hunger, our longing, even (or especially) when we do not feel any kind of fulfilment of that longing, when union seems far from our experience? The longing for union comes from God.

In those times of deep longing which just seem to heighten our sense of unfulfillment and lack of union we are invited to go back to the source. God is the ground of our longing.

> Our Lord wants us to have true understanding, and especially in three things which belong to our prayer.... The first is with whom and how our prayer originates. He reveals with whom when he says: "I am the ground." (chap. 42)

If God is the ground of our longing then we can rest assured that we will experience the consummation. Then after listing the second and third things she concludes,

> And with this intention and for this end was all this loving revealed, and he wishes to help us, and he will make it so, as he says himself, blessed may he be. (chap. 42)

•

Mother Julian is the archetype of serenity. She penetrated beneath the chaos of her world, piercing through the surface anguish, through the deeper despair and cynicism, to the fundamental level and found that the universe is still good, that love surrounds and enfolds us. She saw that we are grounded in God and that God lives in us as in a palace.

We can live as victims if we choose, but we also have the option of choosing to begin to trust love.

This is food for a lifetime. To let go of our cynicism long enough to hear Julian speak what is deepest and truest about us is one of the hardest things we can do.

But at the same time it is like bringing dew to the parched earth of our tragic relationships and broken love. It is like holding one's breath while being transported from downtown Los Angeles to the Sierra Nevadas and then breathing in a whole new world of fresh, invigorating air.

I keep coming back to Julian in my own spiritual pilgrimage as to my motherland. And when I do I realize that when I am alive to this grounding reality of love, I am alive to everything.

Yet, as reassuring as Julian is, I end up wanting more. I want to know something of what this embracing love is. The more I am grounded in the reassurance of love, the more I am restless to know its heartbeat, to be in touch with its energy.

And as I make the transition from trusting love as the true source of my recovery and healing to becoming alive to its pulsating vigor in my life, I am beginning to tap into my passion.

This recovery of passion in the whirl of love between desire for union and the need for individuality is the subject of our next friend from the past, John Ruusbroec.

PART III

John Ruusbroec

Love and Passion

Who then devised the torment? Love.
Love is the unfamiliar Name
Behind the hands that wove
The intolerable shirt of flame
Which human power cannot remove.
  We only live, only suspire
  Consumed by either fire or fire.

— T. S. Eliot, *The Four Quartets*[17]

... love cannot sit idly by but wishes to know and savor thoroughly the fathomless riches which abide in the ground of its being. This is a hunger which is never satisfied. Constantly to strive after something and always fall short is to swim against the stream. One can neither leave it nor grasp it, neither do without it nor attain it, neither speak about it nor remain silent about it, for it is above reason and understanding and transcends all creatures. We can therefore not reach it nor overtake it. We will, however, see into our inmost being, where we will experience God's Spirit driving and enkindling us in the restlessness of love.

—John Ruusbroec, *The Sparkling Stone*[18]

10

The Big Picture

L A S T winter I took up piano lessons again, something I had dropped back in the eighth grade. I not only hated piano lessons, I loved hockey. It was a deadly combination for a thirteen-year-old boy's future with the piano.

Beginning to play the piano again became a real challenge for me. I had been quick to tell my daughter, Nikki, how it was supposed to be done, but could I do it myself? It was all going to be part of a mid-life celebration of a side of me that was never developed.

I tried playing pieces, and I attempted improvising. But try as I might I could not seem to do what I wanted to do, and I became increasingly frustrated. How embarrassing!

Finally, I found that I had to go back to the fundamentals of motor control over my fingers, back to playing the basic scales. I found that I could not even play the scales properly!

I could not do two different things at once with my fingers. If it was time to cross over with my thumb in one hand, it suddenly became the time to cross over with both thumbs simultaneously. The very thought of whipping through four octaves of scales like my fifteen-year-old daughter became a feat of major proportions.

It is like a two-part invention by Bach. I now have a completely different appreciation for those innocent little pieces. Each hand must be able to play independently of the other if the exchanges between them are to become beautiful music.

Once the fingers begin to operate in an independent yet harmonious whole, one other ingredient is needed to make it sound the way Glenn Gould made Bach sound. Bach has to be played with passion. Technical competence alone makes a two-part invention incredibly boring. Passion makes the independent parts sing to each other, it brings the music to life.

This twofold movement is like a dance in which each partner has his or her own unique part, and yet the part itself becomes part of another, a larger whole.

John Ruusbroec, our second writer from the fourteenth century, is the master of the dance. He helps us see that love, like one of Bach's inventions, is the passionate interplay of two independent movements. Ruusbroec gives the whole picture, Eckhart and Dante will each develop one of the movements in detail.

Of all the writers encountered in this book, Ruusbroec (often spelled Ruysbroeck) is the least known, and perhaps the most difficult to read. Most have never heard his name and certainly do not know how to pronounce it! (try something like "Roos' bruck"). He has been a hidden gem lost in our communal memory.

It is to this Flemish mystic that Evelyn Underhill turned in her classic work, *Mysticism*, when she was describing the life of union with God at the very heart of our Christian experience.[19] It was Ruusbroec whom she described simply as "One of the greatest — perhaps the very greatest — of the mystics of the church."[20]

He strained at the outer edges of human spiritual experience seeking to know and describe the essence of mystical union with God. Ruusbroec, more than any other writer before or after, synthesized the streams of love into one dynamic whole. He did so by interweaving a passionate view of love with a dynamic view of the Trinity.

If we can come to appreciate the overall picture, we can put the parts into perspective. Without the integration of Ruusbroec, the radical denials of Eckhart, and the daring affirmations of Dante either become nothing more than choices of preference or eventually degenerate into deviations.

The *New Catholic Encyclopedia* sums up the essential genius of

Ruusbroec by saying that he "tells of the anguish and contention in the soul striving to cross the threshold of time into the eternity from which God calls to it, but coming to accept and welcome this agony as a precious gift from the Lord."[21]

We do not know much about his life. It is not necessary. We know that he became an Augustinian monk and was active in parish life until his fifties. He longed for greater solitude, and with two others he left the parish ministry in March of 1349 and withdrew to a monastery in the forest near Groenendaal, near Brussels in what is now Belgium. He lived there for the remaining thirty years of his life, and it is from this period that his writings emerged.

The writings he left behind do not make for easy reading. As is so often true with writers from another age, we have to be willing to give up some things in order to receive what they have to offer.

In the case of Ruusbroec's vision of love, we have to be willing to grapple with how little the words *love* and *trinity* mean to us. We have become desensitized to both. He fills both full of meaning through the interpenetration of one with the other so that the idea of trinity comes alive in love and love comes alive in trinity.

Ruusbroec is central to the message of this book, because he gives love its fullest possible definition. That definition includes three significant themes. First of all love has to do with union and oneness. Love's second theme is the celebration of diversity and individuality. Finally, the third great theme of love in Ruusbroec's description is the passion that fuels both paradoxical desires for union and for individuality.

These elements comprise an overarching view of love rooted in the heart of the universe, the Trinity. Defining love in relation to the Trinity gives an adequate basis for what we intuitively experience. It gives love a home big enough to encompass the whole. It gives us the freedom to explore the rich complexity of love.

I am well aware that for many people today any definition of love in religious terms is suspect. They are afraid of the possible overlays. Conversely, there are many books out today on love and intimacy that seek to give guidance as to how intimacy works. "How to" books speak of what is constructive and what is destructive to true intimacy. In many cases they are right. They have discovered intuitively or experientially the intricacies of the dance of love.

The point that is consistently missing, however, is an adequate basis, a big enough ground for what is being said. Where is that grounding to be found? How do we know whether it is consistent with love to create boundaries and to pursue one's own individuality? Is some passion good and some bad? How do we know?

I was told before I got married that love in marriage is not fifty-fifty, it is giving 100 percent and expecting nothing in return. Whatever I got in return was then "gravy." Was I to buy that definition? Would it be better to say that marriage is a prenuptial contract in which we negotiate safeguarded protections and services? These questions are not abstract, philosophical questions about the nature of love. They are the questions we agonize with every day of our lives in seeking to live out love in our world.

By using the word *trinity,* Ruusbroec was expressing what he understood to be the very heart and soul of the universe. In so doing he offered to the world a vision of love that is consistent with how the universe is made.

Those who do not want to deal with the religious or theological overtones to the word *trinity* can still find in Ruusbroec a validation of their experience. His description of the Trinity is, in the final analysis, simply a description of the way things are. As you interact with his material, you can see in the notion of a trinity a way of picturing the Reality that fills the universe. You are free to decide whether or not it is a vision of love and the universe big enough and whole enough for you to pursue.

For those who long to integrate their Christian faith with their experience, Ruusbroec's achievement stands as one of the highwater marks in Christian thought. He has taken love back to its source in God, and in so doing has validated for all Christians a full vision of love, a vision that incorporates all of who we are, and the whole of our complex desires.

Julian of Norwich opened the door to trust again, reminding us that love is deeper than evil. If she has made us restless to share in the heartbeat of love that suffuses our world, if we ache to come alive to its pulsating vigor, then we are ready to encounter another of the great writers from the fourteenth century. We are ready to respond to the vision of love as a storm that threatens to consume us in its passion. We are ready for John Ruusbroec.

Before turning to Ruusbroec's writings directly, we will look in the next chapter at the roots of our own loss of love and passion. Then we will be prepared to see how Ruusbroec brings to us a full vision of love as the essential life of the Trinity.

11

Love and the Loss of Passion

L E T ' S be honest. The word *love* is banal. It is so crippled there is almost no possibility that it will be heard without being grossly misinterpreted.

Love has been sentimentalized, trivialized, and eventually perverted into biology and pornography. Is love a rush of warm feelings for a person that I perceive might comfort and protect me? Is love the biological function of sex, the more exotic the performance the more loving it is?

Who knows? And finally, tragically, for too many today, who cares? The breakage experienced in love pushes people to give up on any positive vision of love and to settle for whatever is available or to search endlessly for an unrealistic hope of fulfilment.

This is one great evidence that we have lost our passion. We have become cynical at the point of our greatest potential.

However, if one were to dig deeper one might discover that love is suspect precisely because it names something beyond us. It calls us to something more, to live and grow and become whole. It points to our poverty and makes us own up to how little we truly know about love and intimacy.

But the sentimentalists and the materialists are not the only ones who have trivialized love. Religion, too, has often domesticated love into safe, manageable definitions and moralisms. I grieve deeply when I contemplate how much the vitality of life has been lost to safe religious views of love.

It was common in the Christian circles in which I grew up to reduce love to a discussion of the distinctions between the three Greek words for love: *agape* (self-sacrifice), *phileo* (familial affection), and *eros* (passion). By dissecting the word into discrete categories it was possible to eliminate the dangerous and end up with an innocuous but religiously acceptable ideal of love. Seen this way love became tame at best and hopelessly guilt producing at worst.

Agape was heralded as the real Christian word for love. It was seen as the highest form of love, carrying the idea of self-sacrifice for another's good. There is no doubt that the biblical writers took the word *agape* and filled it with new significance. They saw it as the manifestation of God's love for us in stooping to meet us in our need.

However, they never saw it in isolation. When seen by itself, *agape* takes on a legalistic character. It is not measured by its passion or affection. We do not have to like the people we love, we are commanded to love them by "laying down our lives for them."

Jesus' command, "Love your enemies," is seen as the ultimate standard or test of *agape*. As a Middle Eastern riddle, it is fruitful for meditation. It challenges our categories until we break through beyond definition to a deeper reality. As a definition of love, it is demoralizing for guilt-ridden or codependent people.

Eros has been the real suspect. It is the energy of attraction and the passion for union and fruition. Eros is everywhere in the universe. To come alive to the world beyond our cerebral cortex is to be bombarded with eros. But its emphasis on attraction and passion is so easily deemed primitive and dangerous. It is earthy and therefore not spiritual. In my background it was worldly; passion was simply excluded.

Eros eventually won its place in those circles. It was declared acceptable in marriage. With that clarification, the market was beset, in the 1970s, with evangelical Christian books on marriage which extolled the sanctity, the beauty, and even the exercises necessary for vibrant sex.

Yet these same Christian sex manuals made it clear that passion is out of place outside of marriage. We were to be erotic only in the bedrooms of our marriages.

This view of eros is safe. And it seems to hold the best of both worlds. It affirms a definable moral stance and at the same time allegedly affirms the passion.

Unfortunately, it does not cover all the bases. It does not, for example, address all the unmarried and formerly married people in our society and churches. Are they excluded from passionate love?

Also unfortunately, at least for me as a married person, I don't work that way! And I suspect that most other people don't either. I do not have a toggle switch which allows me to turn amorous desire on and off at will — passionate inside the home and platonic as soon as I open the door to leave the house.

This does not mean that I advocate promiscuity. Rather, it is the best safeguard against promiscuity. If I am aware of my sexuality and learn to live with it in healthy ways, I will not be taken by surprise as a slave to its demands. For better or worse, eros is a part of my total experience of life. I can regard that as a mishap that I must guard against or I can begin to embrace it as part of my vision of love.

Rejecting eros and excluding it from love forces the conclusion that passion is a part of one's sinfulness. It is a problem to avoid. Including it as part of my vision of love means that I must find its good and live that as truly as I can.

And to be honest about it, if one cannot be passionate about life in general, it eventually becomes hard to be passionate about God. What passes for religious passion is often nothing more than projected guilt or a cover for anger and envy. It can be nothing more than perverted passion as truly as alcoholism is a perversion of passion.

Keeping the terms separate allowed people to affirm love without affirming passion. I do not dispute the fact that *agape* is far and away the most commonly used word for love in the New Testament. What I am concerned with is our tendency to compartmentalize these terms until they neatly fit a domesticated, religiously acceptable understanding of love.

Love becomes a kind of bloodless benevolence. It has no passion and no fire. Love becomes a duty, and the command to love one's enemies is either redefined into manageable terms or is used as the final guilt trip to remind people that they have not sacrificed enough yet to live up to what love is.

12

The Passion of Love in the Trinity

RUUSBROEC did not divide love like that. He spoke of the "maelstrom of love" and described it as "flashing like lightning" across our lives. He was at home with passionate desire and with demanding as well as giving. Love is a storm of desire as unsettling as it is inviting.

Ruusbroec's understanding of love and the passion of love in our salvation process is rooted in our conception of the Trinity. And if the word *love* has lost its meaning, what can be said for the word *trinity*.

Now we are in a double bind! We are already dealing with a word full of misunderstanding when we speak of love. Are we going to clarify it by introducing a word not so much misunderstood as not understood at all?

The term "trinity" has very little meaning for us today beyond a religious affirmation. Yes, Christianity is trinitarian. That means that Christians accept a dogma, One God in three Persons.

Christians have become used to distinguishing the three persons in the Godhead and have attached primary responsibilities to each. God the Father is the Creator; "maker of heaven and earth" reads the creed. Jesus is the Savior. The Holy Spirit is the One who indwells and empowers present Christian experience.

Ruusbroec invites us to go beyond a creedal affirmation of the Trinity and to pay attention to that flow of love within the Trinity. It is a dramatic switch from a static view to a dynamic view of the Trinity. It is somewhat like switching from describing a family by its roles to using a family systems model to describe its dynamics. Family systems therapy has helped us to see that the roles are not as important as the dynamic interactions that go on.

To describe the Trinity as One God — Father, Son, and Holy Spirit — names the Trinity primarily in terms of roles. It is like saying I am husband and father, Miriam is wife and mother, and Julie and Nikki are children and siblings. The description is accurate, but it doesn't tell us very much about the family. What goes on between us in the family dynamics is really the essence of the relationship.

Ruusbroec describes the Trinity like a two-part invention. It is a passionate flowing of love which occurs in two simultaneous and continuous directions — inward toward unity and outward toward individuality.

Love as the Movement toward the Embrace of Union

The Trinity is the movement of Persons toward an embrace of love in union so profound and so deep that there are no longer any distinctions between the Persons, only Oneness. At the same time there is a simultaneous and continual flowing out into fruitfulness and diversity or plurality of Persons. It is this ebbing and flowing into union and into fruitful plurality that is the mystery of the Trinity, One yet Three.

Ruusbroec describes this embrace of love as so deep and profound that there are no longer separate distinctions left between the members of the Godhead. He describes it as a union "devoid of particular form," a union so complete that it cannot be determined where one member of the Trinity begins and another ends.

Now this active meeting and this loving embrace [in the Trinity] are in their ground blissful and devoid of particular form, for the fathomless, modeless being of God is so dark and so devoid of particular form that it encompasses within itself all the divine modes and the activity and properties of the Persons in the rich embrace of the essential Unity (p. 152).

The union of God with God is so deep and so full that they are totally and indistinguishably one. Here is the passion of love for embrace, for union, for self-giving. It is the longing of every boy at puberty, to become totally one with the girl of his dreams.

Love as the Movement toward Individuality and Uniqueness

The passion for union is easy to see as love. However (and this is the crucial synthesis that Ruusbroec made), love within the Trinity moves not only in the direction of the Absolute One. Love also moves toward individuality. The union is not a static final experience. It is a fruitful union that bursts forth into the individual persons of the Trinity. Ruusbroec says,

This sublime Unity of the divine nature is both living and fruitful, for out of this same Unity the eternal Word is ceaselessly begotten of the Father. Through this birth the Father knows the Son and all things in the Son, and the Son knows the Father and all things in the Father, for they are one simple nature. (p. 110)

Love, in the Trinity, is both the passion to be One and the passion to be Unique.

This is the other side of love. It is the passion to be a separate individual person. It is the dance of separateness, individuality, and diversity.

The exchange of love in the Trinity is neither the embrace of union so total that there is no distinction left, nor is it the celebration of separate persons. It is both, and *both simultaneously*, each flowing out of the other.

This affects both our understanding of love and our understanding of the pursuit of spiritual experience with God. The goal of spiritual experience, both in Christian terms and in its Eastern forms, has often been expressed as coming to rest in peaceful tranquillity or serenity. It implies being beyond passion.

Quiet is not the goal of Christian spirituality. The quintessence of spiritual experience is to enter as deeply as possible into the simultaneous flowing of love between Unity and Plurality, between losing oneself in union, bursting forth into fruitful uniqueness and losing ourselves again in union.

Love is not confined to self-giving. It includes the experience of validating and celebrating our uniqueness in the flow toward fruitful diversity. Put bluntly, our love is not only what we give but what we crave.

Love as Passion

Passion is a scary word, and linking spirituality with passion is courageous business. If you are like me, you may well ask yourself, "Am I ready for this?" There are many other, more manageable alternatives. Unfortunately it is their manageability that is the root of the sterility that they lead to.

As frightening as the prospect may be, the recovery and transformation of passion is precisely the place of healing from our addictive dependencies and our fearful withdrawal from life. We don't need answers so much as permission. In learning to live constructively with our enthusiastic energy, our creative capacity, our inner longings, and even our grief and anger, we will rediscover a deep richness to our spirituality and will come to freedom in our relationships of intimacy in our world.

Ruusbroec admirably illustrates the reality of passion in love when he describes God's love for us. He is not afraid to say that God is passionate about us, both in the desire to give and in the craving to receive. It is a long passage but well worth quoting.

> The practice of love is free and is not ashamed of itself. Its nature is both craving and generous, for it constantly wishes both to demand and to offer, to give and to take. On the one hand, God's love is full of craving, for it demands of the soul all that it is and all that it can do. For its part, the soul is rich and

generous, ready to give to love's craving all that it demands and desires, but it cannot do this fully, for its created nature must remain forever. . . . On the other hand, God's love is also fathomlessly generous. It reveals and offers to the soul all that it is, and it wishes to give all of this freely to the soul. For its part, the loving soul is now especially gluttonous and full of craving, opening itself in the desire to possess everything which is revealed to it. But since it is a creature, it cannot devour or grasp the immensity of God. (p. 245)

Passion to give oneself away and the craving to receive, the longing for union and the desire to be a unique individual are all the expression of Trinitarian love. They are all to be honored in our experience as the presence of God's life within us. What we do with that passion is another question. That will be addressed by Eckhart and Dante. However, it is essential first that we accept it. The passion for union and for individuality is to be welcomed as part of our spiritual experience.

Trinitarian Love and the Created Universe

If we take this one step further as Ruusbroec does, we can then see how powerfully it affects our vision of love and passion.

This ebbing and flowing of passionate exchange is not a description restricted to the Trinity. It describes the entire universe also. For Ruusbroec this constant movement of love toward essential unity and toward fruitful distinction is the very environment or ground in which the universe as we know it was created. Ruusbroec says,

In this same Unity, considered now as regards its fruitfulness, the Father is in the Son and the Son in the Father, *while all creatures are in them both.* (p. 148)

Ruusbroec is simply suggesting that all separate creatures in the universe find their source in this same ebbing and flowing of love within the Trinity between Unity and the distinction of Persons. He goes on to say that the origin of the universe is found in this bursting forth into distinction between the Father and the Son.

> ... the Son, who is the Father's eternal Word, goes forth as another Person within the Godhead. *Through this eternal birth all creatures have gone forth eternally before their creation in time.* (pp. 148, 149)

And again,

> In this embrace in the Unity all things are brought to their perfection; in the outflow of love all things are accomplished; and in the living, fruitful nature all things have their possibility of occurring.... But as the Persons proceed outward in distinct ways, then the Son is from the Father and the Holy Spirit is from them both; it is here that God has created and ordered all things in their own essential being. (p. 263)

Although Ruusbroec may not be easy to read, what he is saying about the two simultaneous movements of love is a simple but profound notion. It is this paradox between individuality and union that makes love passionate and complex.

We enter the world bursting with the erotic longing for union, a union so deep that we want to be totally lost in the one we love, so complete that we are consumed by each other. We lose this sense of union at birth and spend the rest of our lives looking for it again.

At the same time we have a constant inner surging to be our own person and to assert our own independence in the world. There is a great drive to be seen and acknowledged as someone unique and special. Both of these movements are the expression of love in our lives.

We can begin to see how Ruusbroec enriches our view of love. First he locates love in the very essence of life, in the very ground of creation, in the Trinity itself. This love flows as a passionate yearning for unity and for individuality. Both are necessary for love to exist.

This passion is a movement into profound unity which he calls a bare, imageless abyss of essential Unity. It is characterized by rest, yet it is not static. It is also a fruitful union for out of its depths comes the eternal birth of the Word (the reality of Jesus as a distinct person in the Trinity) in an outward flowing toward plurality and distinction.

In this outward flowing the Son is distinguished from the Father and the Spirit is the love that interpenetrates and flows between the Father and the Son. This flow then moves in attraction toward union again as Father and Son embrace in love and merge into the oneness of their essential unity.

In his own words, "In this meeting between the Father and the Son there arises the third Person, the Holy Spirit, who is the love of them both" (p. 151). This amazing description is not a devaluation of the Holy Spirit but a deepening of our understanding of love. The love that flows between the members of the Godhead is so full and so complete that it can be seen as one of the Persons of the Godhead.

Further, Ruusbroec saw that the entire universe is grounded in that flow of love. Nature finds its source of being in the eternal birth of the Word. Our understanding of our world around us is deepened by our understanding of the Trinity. Our universe, our lives, are full of longing to be seen and known as unique and at the same time to give our selves away in union with another.

Living with the Passion of Love

Perhaps the most revolutionary way Ruusbroec changes our perception of love is that he challenges the common view that love is only self-giving. The person that gives himself or herself away the most is seen as the most loving. The wife that constantly denies her own personhood to meet her husband's demands is seen as fulfilling the Christian ideal of love.

Seeing love as self-sacrifice colors many people's picture of someone like Mother Teresa. She is seen as a hero of love. And she undoubtedly is. However, if she is seen as a hero of love only because people perceive that she cares so little for herself and gives herself away so completely, it is not a healthy picture.

Mother Teresa, herself, talks about her own grounding in the eucharist and how that place of individual affirmation becomes the means by which she can continue giving the way she does.

When self-sacrifice is the sole criterion, it distorts one's perception of love. It leaves out the other side of love, the places where one receives his or her own sense of uniqueness and identity. For the rest of us, it means that we have to "up the ante" and start giving more of ourselves away.

Such a scenario does not bode well for a codependent person. People are codependent because they have come to allow another person to control their life. Many codependent people have grown up believing that their only choice in life is to give up care for themselves and to "sacrifice" themselves for everyone else.

It becomes destructive to their own participation in love. Somewhere the cycle has to be broken or the person will eventually be beaten to a pulp by life and will either check out completely or move away from intimacy simply out of self-preservation.

Love cannot be simply self-sacrifice. Love is an exchange. People in recovery have learned this the hard way. But many recovering from dysfunctional relationships feel that the movement to establish their own personhood and create personal boundaries is contradictory to love.

This movement to individuality feels necessary for survival, but at the same time it seems to violate their understanding of love. These people are put into a real but unnecessary bind.

Seeing love rooted in the Trinity gives people the much needed permission and courage to build their own sense of individuality as part of their growth in love. If the universe is rooted in the love of the Trinity, then we are experiencing the impulse of love when we desire to make ourselves known in the world, to declare our own distinction and uniqueness, and to form our own ego boundaries.

This interplay of desire for union and individuality is part of the very fabric of life. We see its expression at all levels of society. Sometimes it seems like the source of all conflicts rather than evidences of love! Yet the struggle that it presents is itself an evidence of the storm of love and therefore of the presence of God in our lives. It is the arena of our growth into the truth of love.

At the political level, the tension that exists between individual rights and social rights, between the politics of the individual and the state is basic evidence of the presence of love. Does the state take precedence over the individual or vice versa?

It may be true that the movement of love in each of these examples is so distorted that the response becomes one of violence between people or nations, but the passion which underlies the violence is the passion of love gone astray.

Such tensions exist also in the micro experiences of our lives. Perhaps nothing is more raw in marriages today than the seeming

contradiction between what is good for the individual and what is
good for the couple.

Does it take love to work through that dilemma? Yes, of course
it does. But there is more, and the more is incredibly good news.
The very tension itself is witness to the presence of the Trinity and
the grounding of our lives in Trinitarian love.

Parenting only brings more of the same experience. How do we
help our children develop a healthy self-concept without making
them totally self-centered and narcissistic? On the other hand, how
do we help them learn to fit into a larger world without breaking
their individuality and making them servile to that world?

Where is the balance between individual self-expression and
concern for others?

The list of places where this basic contradiction exists is endless.
But the above examples help to illustrate the fact that our lives are
literally grounded in love, that, as Ernesto Cardenal has said, "to
live is to love."[22]

Ruusbroec was familiar with the tension caused by this dynamic
view of love which he presents. Although he does not elaborate
on the implications of that "contradictory movement" in politics
and the family, he does express the same principle in a person's
own experience of God.

He describes this tension as a "storm of love" that buffets us
and creates a craving that cannot be satisfied. In this storm we long
to be in complete union with God and the Spirit of God longs for
union with us. We want to consume or be lost entirely in God, and
yet because we are finite creatures the infinite love in which we
participate cannot be satiated.

> . . . our spirit is buffeted as in a storm by the heat and rest-
> lessness of love. The more we savor, the greater becomes our
> hunger and desire, for the one is the cause of the other. This
> makes us strive without attaining satisfaction. (pp. 176ff)

He describes the love within the Trinity in similar terms. "Here
the Persons give way and lose themselves in the maelstrom of essential love, that is in the blissful unity, and nevertheless remain
active as Persons in the work of the Trinity" (p. 262). It is a maelstrom swirling between individual uniqueness and mutual union.
It is this very storm that Ruusbroec understands as love. It feels

just the opposite! The storm makes us think that we must be far from love. What seems right is that if we only knew how to love we would solve all these dilemmas and be at peace. The very sense of storm seems to indicate that something still is missing.

"If I really knew about love," my inner critic says, "I would know what to do when it seems that what I need as an individual and what is needed in my marriage are contradictory." In some circles the answer would be obvious. *Agape* love demands that we give up what we think we need in favor of what seems to be needed in the marriage. But to capitulate that easily in the storm keeps us from growing in the reality of love that is passionate both for individuality and for union.

Finally, living the love that is at the source of all life preserves a place for passion. One cannot conceive of the Persons of the Trinity loving in the manner we often describe love. At the baptism of Jesus we are given a glimpse into the passion of love that exists at the core of all existence. Luke says, "a voice came from heaven: 'You are my Son, whom I love; with you I am well pleased.'"

Can you imagine the Trinity loving each other by doing good for the other whether they liked each other or not? Can you imagine the Trinity in a passionless embrace of union? It is impossible. But then we are called to remember that this is the kind of delight and love that God also takes in us.

Ruusbroec uses strong words to describe the love within the Trinity which we experience as we open ourselves to that reality. He says,

> In this formless love we will . . . flow forth and flow out of ourselves into the uncomprehended abundance of God's riches and goodness. In it we will also melt and be dissolved, revolve and be eternally whirled around in the maelstrom of God's glory. (p. 159)

He speaks of being initiated into this love and being afflicted with an insatiable craving for total union with God at the center of life. Such persons, he says, "are the most pitiable people alive for they are afflicted with the disease of bulimia and so are filled with a ravenous craving" (pp. 114, 115). It is a storm of love in which "the heat is so extreme that the exercise of love between ourselves and God flashes back and forth like lightning in the sky" (p. 177).

We do not know that level of passion all the time either for our own independence, for a human lover, or for God. However, Ruusbroec is telling us that when we do experience a surge of passion, even at its deepest and most raging moments, it is part of the passion that is at the core of life; it is part of the passion of God.

Whatever our vision of love is going to be it must be profound enough and gutsy enough to allow the full scope of passion.

Ruusbroec helps us to locate our vision of love in the Trinity. That may seem outmoded or unnecessary in our contemporary world. Yet the reality is that no other grounding for love is sufficient to the demands of a full-orbed vision of love.

Love, as the passionate exchanges within the Trinity, preserves the fact that love is the very ground of our existence. It encompasses the highest ideals in self-sacrifice and the strongest sense of self-worth. Trinitarian love preserves the relation of love to passion and integrates the nurture of personal integrity and uniqueness as an essential part of what love is all about.

What does it mean to live passionately in the movement to individuality and what does it mean to live passionately in the movement to union and self-surrender? Meister Eckhart takes up the theme of coming home to our own uniqueness. His radical and controversial views are a strong and important voice to us as we seek to find the balance between narcissism and codependence. It is to Eckhart that we next turn.

PART IV

Meister Eckhart

Coming Home to Ourselves

To be deprived of a simple object of attachment is to taste the deep, holy deprivation of our souls. To struggle to transcend any idol is to touch the sacred hunger God has given us.

—Gerald May, *Addiction and Grace*[23]

I love the dark hours of my being
in which my senses drop into the deep.
I have found in them, as in old letters,
my private life, that is already lived through,
and become wide and powerful now, like legends.
Then I know that there is room in me
for a second huge and timeless life.

But sometimes I am like the tree that stands
over a grave, a leafy tree, fully grown,
who has lived out that particular dream, that the dead boy
(around whom its warm roots are pressing)
lost through his sad moods and his poems.

—*Selected Poems of Rainer Maria Rilke,*[24]
trans. Robert Bly

13

The Importance
of the Homeward Journey

MEISTER Eckhart cut a radical and controversial figure even during his own lifetime. A German Dominican Friar, Eckhart was in his element both in the dialectic of theological discussion and in the pastoral thrust of preaching.

He was quickly recognized within his own order as having unusual intellectual gifts and was sent to Cologne where he evidently studied under Albert the Great (St. Thomas Aquinas's teacher) and to the University of Paris (where Aquinas taught until his death just a few years prior to Eckhart's arrival). The University of Paris, considered the learning capital of the Western world, was in ferment in the wake of Aquinas's thought.

Between and after his travels to study, Eckhart spent his time in pastoral work, giving sermons and providing spiritual direction to the nuns of various Dominican convents. Ordinary as his vocation seemed, his work was far from prosaic.

Eckhart was breaking new ground. He was one of the truly great seminal thinkers in the history of Western thought. Christian experience and belief had reached a new pinnacle of definition in the writings of Thomas Aquinas. Yet the defining of theology did not answer the deep longings of Eckhart's heart.

Definitions and formulations had been useful, but to cling to them would have meant eventual spiritual and emotional death. Something else beckoned. Eckhart explored the inner presence of God as the "Ground of the soul," an encounter so deep and so personal that it is beyond description. He called his followers to let go of all external experience and come home to God at the center of their being. In so doing he gave us a virtuoso performance of one of the two parts of that great invention we call love.

Rowan Williams[25] described Eckhart as someone mapping the territory of the soul for which he had no vocabulary. Eckhart did not back away from the obvious difficulty presented by his search. He courageously, even recklessly at times, forged new expressions and daring paradoxes, to bring humility to our minds and to point beyond the barrier of human limitations.

Inevitably, when theological precision was a measure of one's loyalty to the institution, Eckhart found himself in trouble with ecclesiastical authorities. He was forced to stand trial for heresy and for promoting dangerous teaching first in Cologne and then before the pope in Avignon.

Before the trial in Avignon was concluded, Eckhart died. The papal letter subsequently sent to Eckhart's archbishop stated that Eckhart had recanted from his positions on his deathbed. This secondhand statement of his retraction says that he deplored what he had written and taught, "insofar as they could generate in the minds of the faithful a heretical opinion or one erroneous or hostile to the true faith."[26] With the retraction, the list of statements for which he had been on trial were condemned. And from that time opinions about Eckhart have been ambivalent.

There is no doubt that he had a profound influence on John Ruusbroec, and through John Tauler and the unknown author of the *Theologica Germanica*, on the reformer Martin Luther himself. There is little doubt, also, that he influenced John of the Cross and others that followed. Yet, despite the acknowledged influence, there has been a profound reluctance to grapple with what this man has to say.

Many reasons could be raised for not bothering with Eckhart today. He has been seen as dangerous, and some may say that if he is controversial it is better to avoid him. This is only compounded in this book by our double jeopardy of having to deal both with translations of his works and with excerpts only.

Others may argue that the whole idea of a journey home to oneself seems to be nothing more than an accommodation to an already narcissistic generation. People are overdosed on "me." Why distort spirituality so that people, already steeped in their own egocentric individualism, can feel good about their self-centeredness?

Many people find looking within for any reason, even to find God, a very frightening proposition. It may not be consciously narcissistic, but it is certainly introspective. There is fear that one's search for God will get lost in the labyrinth of neurotic tendencies that lie within us. How will we ever know if and when we find God?

Yet, even with these reservations, Eckhart's thought is unusually provocative and appropriate for us today. With Eckhart, we discover that the way to wholeness is a radically individual adventure. We must take the lonely road home to the core of our being. There, alone in the darkness of our individuality, we can encounter the true source of life.

That pilgrimage is neither narcissistic nor neurotically introspective. It is the only conclusion possible in the face of the biblical affirmations that Christ dwells within us and that we are born of God. There is no such thing as a borrowed spirituality. Somewhere, sometime, we all have to be alone with ourselves and discover what is truly ours.

Death does us the same service. Confronted with a cancer diagnosis, my wife, Miriam, had to face the possibility of dying. She soon discovered that no one could go with her into that experience. Death's spectre had confronted her with her own essential loneliness. Dealing with her aloneness with God, at night when everyone else was asleep and she lay trembling in fear, enabled her to truly live, whether or not she died from the disease.

•

Looking at some of the reasons why Eckhart is important for today will help prepare us to deal with him more directly.

First, Eckhart speaks pointedly to the struggle with busyness. We are scattered and fragmented, trying to cope with the external demands on our time. In the external chaos of the fourteenth century, Eckhart saw how easily people are addicted to things outside them and how important it is to be rooted in the Life inside us.

Life today has only heightened that need. The daily routine is overheated with activities. People multiply time-saving devices like microwave ovens hoping to get a better handle on their time, but really they only complicate it further. Microwave ovens only free up more time to be fragmented and overscheduled.

It is not a matter of time management. One mother, who has come to me for some time, continues to struggle with how busy she is. She cannot seem to find time to nourish her own spiritual growth. I have a great deal of compassion for mothers with young children. There is often not much time or energy left for anything!

We spoke about finding her nourishment in the things that were a natural part of her life already. But nothing really changed. She kept trying to set better priorities and talked about getting control over her schedule. Gradually, she began to be aware that better time management was not the issue. She was addicted to filling her time with activity. She had lost her center.

Second, Eckhart speaks to our sense of inner emptiness. I am becoming increasingly convinced that this journey into the abyss of our soul is sorely needed for men to reclaim the true goodness of their masculinity.

It is a natural tendency for many men to live more in the external world than in their own center. Men are built to go out of themselves. Their very biology is external. Pleasure for a man is not diffused internally, it is focused primarily in one appendage, a throbbing penis.

Men experience a tremendous drive to attach themselves to another person. Sexual union is a powerful way to ensure that one matters. Promiscuity does not mean that there is no attachment; it just means that the need for attachment is so deep it will seek fulfilment almost anywhere. They do not merely attach themselves to a partner to find meaning; they cling to a partner, any partner sometimes, to find existence.

As I have faced my own journey home and have listened to other men, it seems that there are few things more frightening for a man than to return to himself and find his source of life within. The great intolerable fear is that we will find NOTHING. We could not live with such a consequence. Hence we refuse to come home; we continue to look outside ourselves for life.

Meister Eckhart challenges these fears of internal emptiness which have driven men compulsively outside themselves into work or relationship. To let go of attachment to some external source of being and comfort and to begin to discover one's own inner meaning is to risk our very existence by losing everything. Yet this is the very thing that love is calling us to do. If we are to learn to love, we must learn to play our own part independently. We must live out of our own existence so that love does not become our way of constantly loading others with the burden of providing us with our identity.

Eckhart had the courage to face the emptiness. He was willing to enter into the void of his own center. He discovered that the void is infinity. It is the "Ground of our being."

Many women, too, have found that they are "women who love too much."[27] They have been programmed to take care of their husband and to take responsibility for whatever goes wrong in the marriage.

It is no wonder that finally some women wake up and say, "Enough of this! At least my children grow up. This thing I have for a husband will be a child forever."

But necessary as this homeward journey is, it is still fearful. Codependent people have learned that they count only as they are helpful to others. They do not know meaning except to exist on behalf of others. To begin to assert one's self, to name one's own reality and wishes, pushes all their warning buttons.

To stand up for oneself in a relationship seems to be the opposite of love. It seems self-centered and finally sterile and destructive to the relationship. What is it that will keep this from being one more journey into self-absorption?

Here Eckhart is so valuable. To reclaim oneself is to go to the very center and find one's "is-ness" in the One who is bringing life to birth within. It is to return to the Source of intimacy in order to come back into the world able to experience intimacy with freedom from the ways we load love with our needs and dependencies.

Anything less is just a new round of living out of the projections and needs that drove one out of oneself into dependent relationships in the first place. The mix may be different, but it is still only tinkering with the system. The real need is to discover one's true value and to live there.

Some people find reading Eckhart a great relief. For whatever reason their religious background no longer nourishes spiritual growth. They feel alienated or ostracized. Is their struggle with their religious background a sign of being spiritually shipwrecked? The temptation for these people is to move to the sidelines and give up on spiritual vitality.

Scott Peck observes that skepticism may be a step forward in spiritual development.[28] It may be necessary to lose one's formulations in order to keep from being attached to them and stifle further growth into the mystery of love.

Fourth, Eckhart's emphasis on coming home to our union with God is a much needed clarification for the notion of the "God within" that has been popularized by writers within the New Age movement. It is not that the New Age concept of God within is so wrong. The context is missing.

Without the appropriate context, this notion of God within can easily become nothing more than a justification for one's bid for personal automony. Eckhart speaks out of a radically different context. He uses many of the same words, but what he means when he identifies humans with God and how he proposes that this is to be lived would not be very palatable to many who claim that they are god.

Finally, Eckhart helps to give substance to the current emphasis on getting in touch with our inner child. It is a wonderful concept. Jesus knew of its healing power when he welcomed the child on his knee and said, "Unless you change and become like little children, you will never enter the kingdom of heaven" (Matt. 18:3).

When we think of our child we think of that which is good, unspoiled, open to life and eager to participate. A child is one who engages life directly. Children do not so easily get lost in analysis or in projecting a certain image of themselves to others. To reclaim our inner child is to regain that kind of innocence.

As helpful as the concept of reclaiming the inner child has been to people in their recovery, Eckhart shows us the importance of going deeper into ourselves than to our inner child. There is more. Reclaiming the child within can be an important doorway into the deeper, richer truth that is there for all of us.

As we turn to Eckhart's own writing, it may be helpful to remember that he would not ask that we agree with everything he says. Eckhart, himself, specialized in paradoxes. He would want us to focus not on the actual words as definitive, but to allow them to be poor vehicles, at best, to take us further into the mystery of love in our union with God.

14

Our Essential Ground

MEISTER Eckhart, like his contemporary in England, the unknown author of *The Cloud of Unknowing*, has experienced a revival of interest in our day.

Both writers follow what is known as the apophatic tradition in describing spiritual experience. The word *apophatic* comes from a Greek word meaning "to deny." The apophatic tradition in Christian spirituality emphasizes that great no to secondhand or mediated experiences of God.

A mediated experience of God is any way that God is experienced outside us. It may be the beauty of the created world, the support and friendship of others, Bible study groups, or even the use of reason or language to think about God or to speak about God at all.

Both writers push beyond the boundaries of rational thought. They do not despise knowing through the intellect; they show its limitations. These writers have become like beacons of light to many wanting to maintain their Christian roots but who are unwilling to do so in the terms often dictated by a Christianity stuck in idolatry to theological propositions.

The author of *The Cloud of Unknowing* says it in the clearest possible terms when he introduces his method of contemplative prayer.

> All rational beings, angel and men, possess two faculties, the power of knowing and the power of loving. To the first, to the intellect, God who made them is forever unknowable, but to the second, to love, he is completely knowable, and that by every separate individual. So much so that one loving soul by itself, through its love, may know for itself him who is incomparably more than sufficient to fill all souls that exist. This is the everlasting miracle of love."[29]

Meister Eckhart is even more radical. He distrusts even the distinction between knowing and loving and the debate as to their relative value. He maintains that we have the capacity to experience life deeper even than our awareness of knowing or loving. He says,

> In which of these does blessedness consist? . . . I say that *it does not consist in either knowing or loving, but that there is that in the soul from which knowing and loving flow:* Whoever knows this knows in what blessedness consists. . . . So I say that a man ought to be established, free and empty, not knowing or perceiving that God is acting in him; and so a man may possess poverty. (German Sermon, #52, p. 201, italics mine)

The author of *The Cloud of Unknowing* speaks about knowing God without the medium of images, mental or otherwise, but he does not state expressly where that knowing is to take place. Meister Eckhart pushes the theme further by declaring that it is within us, in our innermost depths, that this "apophatic knowing" takes place.

There is something within us that is beyond even knowing and loving — beyond our intellect and our emotions, and therefore beyond our conscious self. This is the center of our being ("heart" is the biblical term) in which knowing and loving find their source. Eckhart explores this deep center and the encounter with God that takes place there.

We will explore Eckhart's development of this theme in this chapter. His own development does not follow a clear structure. Therefore it will be helpful to use a simple progression of thought to help us keep our bearing. There will inevitably be overlaps simply because it is impossible to reduce these thoughts to neat categories.

God's Being and Our Being

Following the pursuit of God into union, Eckhart emphasizes the essential being of God rather than the characteristics of God that we normally think of — God's love, wisdom, justice. He uses the term "is-ness"[30] as one way to describe this essential being. God does not merely have being, God IS BEING. At other times, in order to preserve a sense of simplicity, Eckhart refuses to give any names at all to describe God.

> You ought to sink down out of all your your-ness, and flow into his his-ness, and your "yours" and his "his" ought to become one "mine" so completely that you with him perceive forever his uncreated is-ness and his nothingness, for which there is no name. (German Sermon #83, p. 208)

There is something about simple "is-ness" that confounds description. If something moves, breathes, gets angry, or procreates, one can then elaborate descriptions based on all these things. Eckhart knows that God is active and can be described in terms of these actions, but there is something more that rings in Eckhart's soul. It is this utterly simple "is-ness" of God.

This profound simplicity of being is not an isolated attribute of God. There is within us, also, something which defies description.

> I have sometimes said that there is a power in the spirit that alone is free. Sometimes I have said that it is a guard of the spirit; sometimes I have said that it is a light of the spirit; sometimes I have said that it is a spark. But now I say that it is neither this or that, and yet it is a something that is higher above this and that than heaven is above the earth. And therefore I now give it finer names than I have ever given it before, and yet whatever fine names, whatever words we use, they are telling us lies, and it is far above them. It is free of all names, it is bare of all forms, wholly empty and free, as God in himself is empty and free. It is so utterly one and simple

as God is one and simple, that man cannot in any way look
into it. (German Sermon #2, p. 180)

Eckhart is speaking experientially. He knows that to talk about
the experience requires words. The words fall short, but the experience itself goes beyond words.[31]

God Within: Our Deepest Ground

God's essential, indescribable being is the womb of our own existence. We may describe ourselves as fully as we wish. We may say
we are outgoing or intuitive or a doer or a hunk! But our deepest
existence is not in any of these things. It is rooted in God's is-ness.
This is the headwater of that great river which we know as life.

As truly as the Father in his simple nature gives his Son
birth naturally, so truly does he give him birth in the most
inward part of the spirit, and that is the inner world. Here
God's ground is my ground, and my ground is God's ground.
(German Sermon, #5b, p. 183)

The prophet said, "Truly you are the hidden God" (Is. 45:15),
in the ground of the soul, where God's ground and the soul's
ground are one ground. (German Sermon, #15, p. 192)

This has immediate and startling implications for our self-
concept. Books on parenting and the building of self-esteem in
children have long told us that a child discovers her image of herself as she sees herself mirrored in the way others respond to her.
If those around her think that she is beautiful and special, she will
come to think of herself that way. If those around her think her a
nuisance, she will begin to stay out of life's way. If she is constantly
criticized, she will grow up self-critical, feeling unacceptable and
unworthy.

We cannot avoid this process of purchasing a reflected self-
concept, either in our own childhood or in the lives of our children.
Unfortunately this very process is a significant part of the reason
we are maimed and broken in our perception of ourselves and
therefore in our longing for love. It makes us victims of others'

opinions of us, opinions which are formed mostly out of their needs and anxieties.

We grow up with an outward orientation. We are touched, held, fed, changed, and hurt all from the outside. It is no wonder that we come to the conclusion that life's essence really comes from outside.

A terrible but necessary conclusion confronts us. If I must find out who I am by looking at the smiles and frowns of those around me, it must be because there is something missing inside.

This deep, unarticulated decision becomes the starting point of dependencies, addictions, and our distorted experience of love. We pursue what appears to give us meaning whether it is a mate, career, control of our environment, or a myriad of creative alternatives.

Elizabeth O'Connor, in her excellent book *Cry Pain, Cry Hope*,[32] has a chapter entitled "Letting Go" in which she describes this awesome reality. "These many years," she says, "I have been working with the theme of 'letting go.' Every day, as well as every new stage of life offers opportunity for that work" (p. 49).

We look, O'Connor says, for something outside us but it never comes. She speaks of the awful pain of looking for a blessing from one's parents. But that affirmation is so often withheld. "Yearning for the blessing never given can keep us forever fixed in the past, forever wanting what was withheld." It is this failure to let go of the blessing which we expected from others and never received that keeps us from running toward life and sends us "limping into each new day" (p. 51).

Elizabeth O'Connor then puts the challenge directly,

> To stand on one's own two feet may be the real work of love. Since there is not an abundance of love in our world, none of us can assume that we have done that work well. If we realized the significance of that achievement, I believe we would pursue our independence with less embarrassment and more commitment. (pp. 52, 3)

What does it mean to stand on one's own two feet? O'Connor's answer plunges us into the mystery Eckhart probed with his discussion of "is-ness" and "ground."

> It means knowing that the answers to one's life lie deep in one's own being. It is believing that within one's own heart

are the intuition and wisdom needed for choosing the way one is to go. It is holding the same belief for another. (p. 54)

Our relationship to this "Ground of our being" within us is a two-way street. Eckhart uses a different word picture to describe each movement.

In God's movement to us, Eckhart speaks of the eternal birth of the Word in the soul. As God encounters us it is a movement to bring to birth God's Life in us. This is the source of the whole of our own life and passion.

This birth is there before we are even conscious of it. It is like a fountain bubbling up from within. In the words of Jesus, it is the living water that flows from our innermost being (John 7:37, 38). We simply align ourselves with what is truly emerging from within. Like Ruusbroec, Eckhart places our own existence within the birth of the "Word." Our existence derives from the existence of the Trinity.

> The Father gives birth to his Son in eternity, equal to himself.
> ... Yet I say more: He has given birth to him in my soul. Not only is the soul with him, and he equal with it, but he is in it. ... The Father gives birth to his Son without ceasing; and I say more. He gives me birth, me, his Son and the same Son. ... In the innermost source, there I spring out in the Holy Spirit, where there is one life and one being and one work. (German Sermon, #6, p. 187)

In our movement to encounter God, Meister Eckhart speaks of "the breakthrough of the soul into God."

> A great authority says that his breaking through is nobler than his flowing out; and that is true. When I flowed out from God, all things said: "God is." And this cannot make me blessed, for with this I acknowledge that I am a creature. But in the breaking-through, when I come to be free of will of myself and of God's will and of all his works and of God himself, then I am above all created things, and I am neither God nor creature, but I am what I was and what I shall remain, now and eternally ... in this breaking-through I receive that God and I are one. Then I am what I was, and then I neither diminish nor increase ... here God is one with the spirit, and that

is the most intimate poverty one can find. (German Sermon, #52, p. 203)

As the Eastern Orthodox writers might describe it, the heart which is the center of a person's being is like the narrow point of an hourglass. It opens outward in one direction into the wide world of experience. In the opposite direction, the center of my being opens inward into the world of eternity, into God.

Oneness with God

Oneness with God is the extraordinary conclusion of Eckhart's description of birth and breakthrough. God is simple is-ness. We share in that indescribable simplicity because our being is grounded in God's being. We do not have independent existence as God does, but our existence is truly grounded in God's existence. God is the womb out of which we emerge into the world of experience. Coming home to our heart eventually brings us to the place where who we are and who God is become indistinguishable. As God comes out of infinity to me and as I move inward from the external world to God, we meet at the foundation of my being in such a simple union that I am one with God and God is one with me. This is the truth of John 17 in which Jesus prays that his followers would be one in the same unity Jesus enjoys with the Father.

> In this breaking-through I receive that God and I are one. Then I am what I was, and then I neither diminish nor increase, for I am then an immovable cause that moves all things. . . . I say more: He gives birth not only to me, his Son, but he gives birth to me as himself and himself as me and to me as his being and nature. (German Sermon #52, p. 203)

The bold, unqualified nature of Eckhart's statements have made many uncomfortable. Actually others, including Ruusbroec and Julian of Norwich, make similar statements about the depth of our union with God, but they are more explicit in the qualification that this does not do away with our finiteness as creatures. Perhaps Hadewijch of Antwerp says it best,

...He shall teach you what He is, and how wonderfully sweet it is for the beloved to dwell in his Love, and how Love so dwells in all the beloved that neither can perceive difference between them. But they possess one another in a mutual possession, their mouths one mouth, their hearts one heart, their bodies one body, their souls one soul, and sometimes one sweet divine nature transfuses them both, and they are one, each wholly in the other, and yet each one still remains and always will remain himself.[33]

Union with God is a biblical theme and one that has been held throughout Christian history. Athanasius penned the famous statement, "God became man that man might become God."

In his letters, Paul makes the same point. To the Colossians he declares that "in Christ all the fullness of the Deity lives in bodily form." Then he goes on, using the same language, to say, "and you have been given fullness in Christ" (Col. 2:9, 10). Paul prays for the Ephesians that in God's love that surpasses knowledge they "may be filled to the measure of all the fullness of God" (Eph. 3:19).

In this union with God, we live out a fullness of life that comes from within because we are one with God. We enter life with the ability to give and to receive with enjoyment. We do not need to demand. Our life and dignity is coming from inside us.

Another important implication of Eckhart's insistence on the reality of God within is that it provides an extremely helpful supplement to the concept of the "inner child" popular in the literature on healing codependency. Eckhart challenges us to remember that while the inner child can be the doorway into our center, it is not the ground of our being.

We cannot stop with returning home to our inner child. First of all, if the inner child is all that is found inside, it still leaves one isolated and alone. There is no final intimacy within if all that we are reclaiming is ourselves.

Second, although the "child within" does portray an image of zestful innocence and can be the place where I find my passion, it also can just as easily portray a sense of dependence, powerlessness and vulnerability. Eckhart calls us home to the simplicity and freedom of the child but he also calls us home to the strength and invulnerability of God. In the words already quoted,

in this breaking-through I receive that God and I are one.
Then I am what I was, and then I neither diminish nor
increase. (German Sermon #52, p. 203)

Finally, Eckhart helps us to bring a needed qualification to the
work of reclaiming and living out of our child. Our child is not
only innocent, it is also narcissistic and self-willed. That is fine
for a child. It is all the child knows. If our inner child is free to
abandon itself to the good, it is also quite capable of demanding
what is immediately attractive but completely unhealthy.

Our child is, in the famous words of Wordsworth, an "inti-
mation of immortality." Our child points us to the possibility of
innocent participation in the world of love. But our child is not the
end in itself. It is the doorway to the fullness of God within.

Letting Go of Attachments

It is somewhat double-edged to discover that life does not come
from outside! It is exhilarating to contemplate the fact that I have
such depth of being that in some indescribable way I am one with
God. On the other hand, the journey to my center requires that I
let go of my persistent belief that I will find my meaning in some
outside person or experience. Returning home means leaving the
"far country."

Detachment is the refusal to buy into any outside experience
as my source of life. It is what Jesus spoke about in the parable of
the person who found a pearl of great price. He sold everything he
had and bought the field.

We said at the beginning of this chapter that Eckhart challenges
the notions, popular in New Age writers like Shirley Maclaine, of
the God within and that we are God.

The words may be the same but the context is very different.
Claiming to be one with God is not an easy identification. Eckhart
put it in a way that would make most people run away. "Who
are they who are thus equal?" he asks. His reply? "Those who are
equal to nothing, they alone are equal to God" (German Sermon,
#6, p. 187).

Meister Eckhart has strong words to say about this process

of letting go in order to return home to our center. In one of his strongest statements about our oneness with God, he concludes by saying, "This is the most intimate poverty one can find" (German Sermon, #52, p. 203).

Obviously for him, oneness with God is not an easy justification for autonomy. It is a source of life and a source of death. It is the guarantee that life will spring out of him and that he will be able to enter into life fully. At the same time it calls for a death to all addictive dependencies that would substitute for that inward grounding.

He speaks often about letting go our attachment to external things in order to sink down into this union with God. When he says "let go" or "go out," he is not talking about some place external to us. He is referring to the infinite depth into which we emerge when we "go out" through the center of our being and emerge into God.

> That is why I say that if a man will turn away from himself and from all created things, by so much will you be one and blessed in the spark of the soul.... This spark rejects all created things, and wants nothing but its naked God. (German Sermon, #48, p. 198)

His views of detachment have sometimes been taken to mean that he made a dualism between the spiritual and the material worlds and rejected any sensual experience as evil. Eckhart is not denying the external world, nor is he denying enjoyment of the goodness of life. But he is making sure that we know who we are first.

Even the phrase "let go" has often carried oppressive religious baggage. It has, for many, meant that in order to be truly spiritual one must give up one's favorite pleasure as some kind of sacrifice to God. There is certainly a place for voluntary asceticism in our time. But most of us do not have to create places to "let go." They are raised in abundance by life itself and the relational struggles that are part of our chaotic existence.

"Sink down" is a much more lively image. It does not imply struggle with an external deity who has grabbed our "favorite toy" and demands that we let go. It is the simplicity of relaxing into God. There is nothing more simple than sinking down.

You ought to sink down out of all your your-ness, and follow into his his-ness. (German Sermon, #83, p. 207)

Eckhart offers two illustrations to indicate what he means. First he says that this kind of detachment releases a person from prejudice toward those who are different. We tend to prefer people who are similar to us. When I am free of attachment to people being like me, I am free to love people as they are, not as they fit into my life and my needs.

Whoever is to remain in the nakedness of this nature without any medium must have gone out beyond all persons to such an extent that he is willing to believe as well of a man far beyond the seas, whom he has never set eyes on, as he does of the man who lives with him and is his closest friend. (German Sermon, #5, p. 182)

His second illustration deals with prayer.

People often say to me: "Pray for me." Then I think: Why do you not stay in yourself and hold on to your own good? After all, you are carrying all truth in you in an essential manner.... That we may so truly remain within, that we may possess all truth, without medium and without distinction, in true blessedness, may God help us to do this. (German Sermon, #5, pp. 184, 185)

The reference to prayer is particularly telling because it helps explain how to interpret Eckhart's words. Eckhart has put the matter in absolute terms. It goes without saying that Eckhart did not reject all external forms of prayer to God. He is challenging the way we can become addicted even to religious disciplines.[34]

We cannot achieve this letting-go process through our own efforts. Eckhart uses a paradox to illustrate his point. He says that as long as we are trying to achieve this simple union, this "nothingness," we will never get there.

So long as "nothing" holds you bound, so long you are imperfect. Therefore, if you want to be perfect, you must be naked of what is nothing. (German Sermon, #5, p. 183)

But we can sink down.

15

Spiritual Homecoming

THIS profound homecoming into an unknowable union with God has enormous implications for our spirituality and our notions of God.

Picking up on a quote from Augustine, "The best that one can say about God is for one to keep silent out of the wisdom of one's inward riches," Eckhart suggests that we should stop chattering about God and trying to understand God. "Then how should I love God?" he asks.

> You should love God unspiritually, that is, your soul should be unspiritual and stripped of all spirituality, for as it has images, it has a medium, and so long as it has a medium, it has not unity or simplicity. Therefore your soul must be unspiritual, free of all spirit, and must remain spiritless; for if you love God as he is God, as he is spirit, as he is person and as he is image — all this must go! "Then how should I love him?" You should love him as he is a non-God, a nonspirit, a nonperson, a nonimage, but as he is a pure, unmixed, bright "One," separated from all duality; and in that One we should eternally sink down, out of "something" into "nothing."

May God help us to that. Amen. (German Sermon, #83, p. 208)

Although it sounds intimidating, when we actually begin to face it, this movement away from images and conceptions of God to a dark, direct union with God is not as unfamiliar as one may think.

It names what many people in our time have been forced to experience, whether they intended to or not, in relation to their own church tradition. People who have been alienated from their own religious tradition have had to come to terms with their own spirituality without the support of the church or what they understood the church taught.

For example, many divorced Catholics have gone through the experience of feeling unwelcome in their own church. They became religious pariahs when their marriage failed.

Many women in the church feel the same alienation. Their gender has been enough to exclude them from ministry and made them experience difference rather than union with God. They have been forced to find ways of experiencing God that validates their own being whether or not their church supported that journey.

People from my own fundamentalist Protestant background speak to me about their struggle, at great cost, to come to terms with their individual spiritual experience. It gradually became evident that the religious outlook they had grown up with was too narrow and death producing to encompass the fullness of the world and of God.

It is probably safe to say that most, if not all of us, at some time or other, especially in the transition era that we are now in, will have to go through some sense of loss of our familiar image of God. We will have to embark on a journey into an unknown, toward the One we can no longer name in order to deepen our spiritual experience.

To refuse the journey is to end up in a religious death — all the parts intact but the vitality gone. Many of us desperately need permission to make the passage from conceiving of God exclusively outside, operating externally on my world, to God within, emerging into my world from the depths of my being. It is the change from talking about God to being at home with God inside.

It is profoundly frightening to move away from the known

images of God and surrender in love to God beyond one's images. It is like shaking one's very core of belief and existence. But we soon discover that there is no other way. There is no shortcut, no "plan B." One's spirituality has been defined by external rituals, activities or people. Now defining spirituality externally no longer fits. It is a time of real crisis.

Sr. Nora, my first spiritual director used to say to me, "There is no other way through the tunnel but through it." Only the bright smile on a face lined with pain encouraged me to believe that she knew what she was talking about.

Eckhart speaks of the journey from duality to union, not from duality to isolation. We fear that to stand alone with God in a way that depends neither on any outside source or even on our rational conception would be to stand in total isolation. The very opposite is true.

When we finally let go of all the support systems we have built up to explain our world, including our theological propositions and systems of belief, we find that eventually we experience a union that is beyond description. We have been so busy looking outside for the essence of life, even for God, that we have neglected the fundamental truth that God meets me at the core of my being, in my "heart."

This journey calls us to what I have come to describe as passionate agnosticism. That is not an oxymoron. There is no contradiction in terms here.

Agnosticism is usually associated with removal from active participation into the role of an observer. Passionate agnosticism is the process of letting go our preconceived notions of God, not to get away from God, but to run wide open into God. There is no backing away from participation. It is a deeper and more passionate plunging into the reality of God, even though there is no longer any way to describe or define it.

One of the most frequent stories I hear is a tearful, sometimes angry story that one's own belief system has been lost. That which previously nourished them spiritually no longer brings life. What can they do? Must they give up on spirituality? What does their spiritual journey now look like?

They are being called to a deeper experience of union. It is really growth. The journey is painful, but Eckhart reassures us that it will not be futile. We can trust that the core of our being is filled with God.

In this paradox of sinking down into indescribable union, Eckhart also speaks to the contemporary notions of self. Sinking down into one's true self, into God, relativizes one's notions of self-concept, whether borrowed from others or constructed on one's own.

In coming home to myself, I go through the process of reclaiming the parts of myself that I have given away. Part of that process includes the solidification of self. This includes the creation of boundaries where others have had the habit of violating my person. It also includes welcoming my shortcomings and my gifts.

A woman learns to accept the fact that she is not a detailed person and that her housekeeping will not reflect a nicely organized existence. A man learns to accept the fact that he has strong nurturing qualities that are usually associated with being feminine. A woman chooses to refuse to let her husband shame her anymore by calling her names. These are all examples of developing a solid sense of self.

However, Eckhart reminds us that in reclaiming or naming our "self" we have gone only half way. If we are going to find our real "identity," we will eventually sink beyond any notions of self-concept.

It is an amazing paradox. Here the journey finally moves from reentering my "self" to abandoning "self" beyond self. The loss of self that Eckhart calls for is through coming to the center of myself. Here I am most truly myself and at the same time most free of limited notions of self. James Houston speaks about this paradox.

> Then an amazing paradox begins to dawn upon me: that I am never more truly myself than when I have given myself up to God. My actions are never more truly authentic than when they are the Spirit's actions through me.... God has most glory before the world when I am most genuinely human.[35]

To cling to a particular definition of who I am at this point only hinders further sinking into the true center of my being. Here with God I experience a radical union. But as Ruusbroec emphasized the union is fruitful. The ongoing union gives ongoing birth to a creative individuality with which I reemerge into the world. I enter life bringing with me the riches of the infinity of God.

Borrowing a quote, Tilden Edwards makes this point in his book *Spiritual Friendship*. Having described Jesus as one who was always receiving his "self" from God, he says, "Our identity in Christian tradition therefore is not some hard 'possession' to find and clutch. It is a continually unique gift that by its very nature is unpossessible, only shareable."[36]

It is a fine irony! Not only do we lose our ability to define God, we also lose our ability to define ourselves! We no longer need to pigeon-hole ourselves. We are whatever God is emerging from within us. This is true freedom.

Eckhart has pushed the one direction of love to the deepest possible place. The recovery of love inevitably calls us away from our addictive and dysfunctional dependencies. There is only one place to go. We must find God within us. There in the unfathomable depths of our union with God we learn that we can live out of our center. We can tap into the Source of our life and return to relationships and living with passion gifted with a healthy sense of independence and individuality.

Dante, will take us in the opposite direction. He will draw us outside ourselves. He will help us affirm the glory we experience in seeing God present in the world around us. Through the affirmation of our passion, aroused by the potency of our longing, we will discover the glory of passionate exchange and become part of the great dance that energizes the entire creation.

PART V

Dante Alighieri

The Glory of Passionate Exchange

God is not always silent, and man is not always blind. In every man's life there are moments when there is a lifting of the veil at the horizon of the known, opening a sight of the eternal. Each of us has at least once in his life experienced the momentous reality of God. Each of us has once caught a glimpse of the beauty, peace and power that flow through the souls of those who are devoted to Him. But such experiences are rare events. To some people they are like shooting stars, passing and unremembered. In others they kindle a light that is never quenched. The remembrance of that experience and the loyalty to the response of that moment are the forces that sustain our faith.

—Abraham Heschel[37]

16

Awakening

DANTE'S great epic, *The Divine Comedy*, opens with these arresting words,

> Midway this way of life we're bound upon,
>   I woke to find myself in a dark wood,
> Where the right road was wholly lost and gone.

> (*Hell*, canto i)

It is a tragic beginning. He is, at midlife, just beginning to wake up. The Italian is even stronger, "I came to myself."

The reality he faces is dark and foreboding. Here, as the scene opens, Dante is lost, and the goal of love seems to be a distant and unattainable pot of gold at the end of the rainbow.

The Divine Comedy is a mythic story of Dante's journey from addiction to freedom, from dysfunction to love. It begins with his own brokenness, and he chokes for words as he attempts to get the story out.

> Ay me! how hard to speak of it — that rude
>   And rough and stubborn forest! The mere breath
> Of memory stirs the old fear in the blood;

> (*Hell*, canto i)

It is painful to come to ourselves and acknowledge how badly we have been hurt and have hurt others in love. It is painful enough to admit them to ourselves; harder still to speak about them to others.

Who wants to name the pain? I, for one, do not! I do not want other people to know me as the person who does not know how to love, or who was abused in love.

To wake up to our own wounds of love through a broken relationship, to begin to feel the lostness of the ways we keep people from us, to name the pain that sabotages our experiences of love — these are some of the most difficult experiences of our lives. We avoid facing up to the truth of our situation as long as possible.

How often people cling to bits of intimacy, even when it is unhealthy, just to keep from having to deal with how far they are from the ability to love freely. Sometimes, as in the case of sexual abuse, people block their experience out of memory almost entirely.

Yet for many people, telling their own story has become a major part of their healing. Sometimes it is only in the telling itself that the possibility of healing finally breaks out into the open.

Dante continues by recounting that he could see glimpses of the sun shining on the mountain of his destiny (the place where love is experienced passionately and freely), but he was unable to get there.

This confronts Dante with a deeper horror. He is not only lost and afraid, the way to love is barred. He had been grieving the past. Now his eyes have moved to the future. If the past looked tragic, the future looks abysmal. Beyond the bankruptcy of his present experience, Dante awakes to the terror of his future if things don't change.

Dante finds that his way forward is blocked by three animals. These animals symbolize his passion in his youth, middle age, and old age.[38] Try as he might, Dante cannot get past them. The last is by far the worst. He describes it as a wolf "gaunt with famished craving lodged ever in her horrible lean flank." It is the spectre of the unresolved passion projected into old age, never dulled and never satiated.

Clutching a handful of shattered ideals, he is coming to know the terrible agony of unfulfilled longing. Is this all he can expect out of life — an increasing craving for love without any promise of fulfilment?

I suspect that Dante here has touched into the core of one of our greatest fears. We are not a society that knows much about living with unfulfilled longing. The thought of living with passion AND without fulfilment is unthinkable. Either kill the passion or guarantee its satisfaction. We have often been caught between the rock of a religious value which advocates killing the passion and a consumer society hard place which promises universal fulfilment.

•

So begins Dante's great poem of love! As one of the great epic poems of all time, *The Divine Comedy* offers many levels of meaning. We will pursue only one level here, the explicit journey to recover love.

As we acquaint ourselves with *The Divine Comedy* (remember a Comedy is a dramatic play or poem with a positive ending), we will look briefly at Dante's own life. After setting the context for *The Divine Comedy* in Dante's own life, we will seek to discover the essential gift that Dante is trying to offer in writing the *Comedy*. Dante is really only trying to say one great thing. Capturing that overall picture in our hearts will make the details of his journey that much more powerful.

Finally, we will follow Dante through the three stages of his own recovery of love. First, Dante will describe the disintegration process of untransformed passion in hell. We will climb with him up the mountain of purgatory in which desire is brought to freedom. Finally, in paradise Dante will bring us into the mystical union of all things in God.

Dante's Own History

The opening lines of *The Divine Comedy* speak deeply to our own struggles with love. They become even more poignant when we understand how the great epic was born. By looking into Dante's experience, we see more clearly the threads of our own anguish and thereby are able to enter more fully into the vision that he presents of the healing process.

Dante identifies himself as being in that infamous experience we have come to know as mid-life crisis. It is not the brain child of twentieth-century boredom. It is the transition which triggers our awakening process from illusions to reality.

Someone said recently that a person is not on a journey unless there is some spark of recognition of the journey. Anthony De Mello maintains that this is exactly what we do not want to do. We do not want to wake from our illusions, from the semihypnotic state in which we live.[39]

But whether it happens as Dante describes, at thirty-five, when the things in which we have invested the most meaning seem to evaporate before our eyes, or whether it happens to a girl at twenty-one when she realizes that, because of sexual abuse in her past, she is unable to share intimacy with men to whom she is attracted, it is the same awakening process.

There come moments in each of our lives when we begin to wake up to the fact that we have lost our way in love and are caught in a deep forest full of tangled undergrowth. For all our desire for intimacy, we find that we have become lost and enmeshed. We have no idea how to recover from our shattered lives.

Perhaps we have tried to live passionately and it has only taken us into deeper and deeper difficulty. Our resulting addictions have created untold pain for ourselves and others. Or perhaps we have been afraid of passion and have therefore lived tightly controlled lives. But even in our neat little controlled experience we begin to wake up to how deeply that addiction to control has affected our life. We begin to observe just how much of life we have robbed from ourselves and from those around us.

Where was Dante to turn? It was his unique answer to that question that provoked one of the greatest poetic achievements of all time. In his sense of loss and disillusionment, Dante went back to his earliest experience of love to see if it was authentic, if it was, indeed, a pathway to God.

As a boy of nine, Dante attended a neighborhood party. Perhaps he was there just to have fun like all the other boys. He was totally unprepared for what actually happened.

While at the party, Dante looked up, and there before him stood a girl his age looking at him and smiling. He nearly died on the spot. Beatrice "knocked him off his feet!" In that moment he experienced his first rush of sexuality and romance. It was a moment of sheer joy and exquisite suffering!

Dante later described it in three ways.[40] He recalls that his heart said, "Behold a god more powerful than I, who comes to rule over me" (I'm smitten!). His sensory awareness said, "Now your source of joy has been revealed" (this is the best thing that could ever happen!). And his liver (his "gut") said, "Woe is me! for I shall often be impeded from now on" (this is going to be painful!).

Do you remember your own first rush of love, the sense of ultimacy, a sense that the whole world suddenly changed colors? Do you, like me, also remember a simultaneous sick feeling in the pit of your stomach!

It was good while it lasted, right? Full of dreams and possibilities. But we all got over it. That cute, naive experience we so condescendingly refer to as infatuation or puppy love was fine for a young boy, but Dante would grow out of it into maturity in adult life.

Dante did mature. His writings witness to his pilgrimage. His first book, *La Vita Nuova*, is filled with passionate poetry about Beatrice. When he was twenty-five, while writing the book, Dante learned of her death.

In his grief, Dante retreated from passion for romantic love into passion for intellectual achievement. Sound familiar? Brash and gifted, he consumed philosophy and theology, deciding, eventually,[41] to write a book that would be a veritable feast of knowledge. It was called *The Convivio* (banquet) and was to provide a full satisfaction to the human quest for knowledge. *The Convivio* was never finished. It could not be. Dante had to finally give up on another illusion of finding satisfaction to the hunger within him.

Despite his massive intellect, the search to find fulfilment in knowledge was hopeless. In the words of Anthony de Mello, "No one ever got drunk on the word 'wine.' "[42]

Dante's one other great love and hope for meaning was the city. The city represented community. If Beatrice was his own personal image of glory in the passionate exchange of love, the city was the communal image of the exchanges of love given and received among many people. The two cities on Dante's horizon were

Florence, his hometown, and Rome, the center of his Christian faith.

But Rome was suffering unprecedented corruption culminating in the removal of the papacy to Avignon in France, and Florence was torn by civil war between two powerful families. Dante witnessed the relentless demolition of his hopes for a renewed Rome and a revitalization of the papacy.

Compounding the pain, Dante was accused of treachery in his home town. He had become active in the politics of Florence, but while he was away, Dante was accused on trumped up charges of treason. He was banished from Florence for life in 1302, on pain of death. He never returned. Dante died in 1321, in exile, living on the goodwill of friends.

In 1307, at the age of forty-two, five years after his exile, Dante began work on *The Divine Comedy*. He had lost Beatrice, he had discovered the futility of knowledge, his vision of religious community had been shattered and he was now homeless and dependent.

Is it any wonder that he begins with a sense of desperation? Where can he experience life in its true fullness? Eckhart may have said, "Go inside. Abandon the images that have disappointed you so badly and seek God directly in your own soul."

Perhaps we might have said, "grow up. Be reasonable; get on with life and quit being so passionate."

Dante responded differently, and in so doing he provided the second great part of the music of love described by Ruusbroec. Rather than abandon the search for life through passion, Dante chose instead to return to his original experience of passion, his love for Beatrice. He chose to open up to his passion until it unlocked its deepest treasure, until it revealed its own eternal Source, its inherent glory.

Dante's Great Gift

Dante's great gift to our recovery of love is that he offers to us a vision of the potency of life around us. He discovers the presence of God in the world around him just as Eckhart discovered the presence of God within his own soul.

The return home to ourselves calls for a radical transformation; so also the recognition of God in the exchanges of passionate love around us calls for transformation and growth. This growth involves welcoming the potency of our passion for life, letting go of the ways we cling to it and distort it, finding in the passion the freedom to make constructive choices, and finally following our passion to its goal of mystical unity in God.

For Dante, as for many, the way to this growth in love was through a return to the childhood experience of adoration. Children have the wonderful ability, in one fell moment, to be enraptured. A balloon, a toy, or a candy suddenly overwhelms a child's attention. Time vanishes as the child gazes through the portals of this world into a world alive with wonder.

Children have eyes to see beyond the labels we put on things. They see God present, lighting the world with glory and delight. They naturally sense the glory and respond with adoration and desire. They have not yet learned how to hide the passion.

We have the privilege of welcoming this wide-eyed child and incorporating its sense of wonder into our own recovery of love. We never really outgrow our past. Our childhood is as much a part of our present as the inner rings of the tree are part of the tree's present life. We will learn, if we choose to follow, to see our world potent with the passion of love.

This reveals the core of Dante's exploration. Did that original nine-year-old infatuation have credibility? Is the passion for adoration and self-giving a window into eternity? Dante is more specific. Can a romantic or sexual attraction be a doorway into God?

A young boy is love-struck over the girl with the big brown eyes. A little girl adores her strong and friendly teacher. Two adults, each married, discover they have passion for each other. Do these experiences carry the seeds of grace and the presence of divine life? These are the questions Dante poses for us.

We might ask, "Is living passionately a truly viable way of spirituality? Is *amor* (Dante's word for love) to be cherished everywhere, or is it too dangerous for spirituality? Is spirituality about the honoring of, or the policing of, romantic and sexual love?"

Romantic love is not the only possible horizon here; it is only the most controversial. Passion for skiing, golf, or fishing, passion for one's career as a musician or corporate executive, passion for justice, these are all the arena of love. Dante will go further. Passion expressed destructively as wrath or violence is also a doorway into growth and into God. We are invited to go to the roots and discover the truth of love that resides at the core of even the most distorted passion.

Passion is, in its essence, the bubbling up of Divine Love at the center of our being. It is, in the words of Gerald May, "our best gift, our most treasured possession."[43] One of the early church writers spoke of desire as the highway of God into the soul.

Passion does not go away. As in anger, if it is not welcomed it will become devious and find some distorted expression. Choosing to accept the passion, however it comes, without clinging either to the object of the passion or to the need for fulfilment is the way of transformation. Both the moments of union and the moments of unfulfilled longing become great healing gifts.

Accepting the passion unconditionally faces one with the reality of choice. There is no choice if the passion is not received. What, for example, does a person know of moral purity who lived so fearfully that intimacy was never a possibility. Choice becomes a real possibility when longing is accepted and fulfilment is celebrated but not demanded. This is the place of freedom, the place where "all things are yours."

Therefore to categorize passion as dangerous or to squelch it in the name of piety is to thwart the very essence of life with which we relate not only to our outside world but also to God.

Passion must be accepted and honored. Desire and longing must be welcomed unconditionally as a rightful occupant in one's life, before it is crushed with cautions, if it is ever to become fruitful in our spiritual and emotional growth.

Dante's own experience fired the genius of this high vision. He did not have an affair with Beatrice. He married and had children by a woman named Gemma. Beatrice also married. Yet Dante neither denied his love nor demanded its gratification. He followed the passion of adoration to its truth. Had he demanded the fulfilment of his passion through an affair with Beatrice or denied his passion because he was married to Gemma, he might never have composed a poem with the grandeur of *The Divine Comedy*.

Dante helps us to bring our vision of love to wholeness. He encourages us to accept not only the radical denial of all attachments in our return home to ourselves, but also the radical affirmation of the very objects of our passion and of the passion itself. It is the final redemption of the addictive cycle.

17

Hell:

The Journey into Honesty

IT is impossible to encompass seventeen thousand lines of epic poetry here. Yet we can see something of the landmarks and get a feeling for the story of the journey. To see our contemporary intuitions exemplified in a six-hundred-year old story gives us assurance and confirmation, a feeling of being one, not only with the present, but also with our tradition.

Almost invariably, in our awakening to the sweet revelry of passion we are also awakened to how poor we are at living well with our passion.

We think we are reaching out for the most in life, but in reality we are settling for too little. In the words of one writer we settle for being red hot in our passion rather than becoming white hot with love.[44]

William Blake reminds us that if our perception were cleansed we would "see everything as it truly is, infinite." We naturally learn the opposite. We learn to see things not as they truly are but what they might be for us. Everything is evaluated unconsciously by a single criterion: How will I benefit?

Dante sees Beatrice as the revelation of glory. At first that sense of glory is dominated by his own needs. He sees her through the lens of what she represents for him, the fulfilment of his projected image of his love. It is the first great moment of choice. Will Dante cling to his own perception or will he let love show him the way to freedom?[45]

The descent into hell is the interior journey that we must all make into our souls. It is the honesty to refuse to project onto others one's own needs and struggles. It is the gradual recognition of how a person distorts the very love that he or she wants to affirm.

We must go down into the pit to look at the end result of untransformed desire. We will probably want to hold our nose and close our eyes. But that is precisely what we dare not do. One cannot afford to respond like a middle-class tourist passing through the slums. We dare not deny what is truly ours to own. This is our story, not the story of some poor victim or some lazy devil who knew better.

Hell is the refusal of choice. It is the refusal to choose transformation. Or we can say that it is the unmitigated choice to cling to our illusions and to become victims of passion rather than discover the truth of love inherent in our desire.

But the choice to demand that I have it my way is finally an abdication of choice. The alcoholic who adamantly chooses to continue drinking eventually ends up without the choice to stop.

The refusal to confront one's marriage partner out of fear of conflict leads one eventually to a living hell in which nothing difficult is confronted and nothing positive is lived.

Clinging to an illusion of objective detachment and cool rationality leaves us sucked dry of vitality. These are the infernos we know about.

Most of us, if we know anything about Dante, know about his gruesome descriptions of the tortures in hell. He is often unfairly depicted as someone with a sadistic streak that loved to paint the most sordid pictures of damnation by an angry God. His is the cruellest possible description of a judgmental God, the very paradigm of an abusive spirituality. It is just the sort of religion we want so badly to be liberated from.

It has been a gross offence to read what Dante saw inscribed over the gateway to hell, "Abandon all hope all ye who enter here."

But Dante's statement is not lightly made. Nor does it describe God's spiteful vengeance. It is a statement of simple reality for those who choose to live the hell he describes.

Dante's description of hell is a vivid picture of an addict who persists is his or her own form of dependency. It is the story of everyone who has lived the first step of the twelve-step program, "I admitted I was powerless over (my addiction) and that my life had become unmanageable."

In that sense there is no hope for those in hell. To persist in one's own perverted choice is to leave out any room for change, and the very thing that appeared so life-giving, so full of potential at the beginning, now takes on a monstrous and destructive life of its own.

Once seen in its more extreme context of addiction, it can been recognized as an integral part of our growth. When we come to know in painful honesty the enormous costs of our unwillingness to deal with our addictions and dependencies, we will have no trouble hearing Dante's description. We know only too well the downward spiral from passionately sweet but untransformed love to the frozen wastelands where the ego is so self-centered that no exchange, even distorted exchange, is possible anymore.

As we travel with Dante through hell, purgatory, and paradise, it will be helpful to recognize that Dante is not simply giving vivid descriptions of life after death. As in Greek mythology, Dante projects into the afterlife the personal journey that we all experience in this life.

There are at least two great advantages to this. The first is that it removes the story far enough away from direct experience that it can be looked at with a more objective eye.

Second, by projecting the story into a final state, everything is seen as a kind of snapshot. Dante's own story is the only one that moves forward. Everyone else remains static and that provides a clearer way to look at his own experience.

Dante is the one called to change. He must take ownership for his own story and his own transformation process. He knows and models what we have come to know in recovery, that I can only change myself.

Shortly after the story opens, Dante discovers that hell is a downward spiral. A hole has been made in the earth through the fall of Lucifer and it extends downward in increasingly narrow circles until it reaches the very center of the earth.

Dante continually bombards the senses with the impression of increasingly constricted and claustrophobic space. The space grows narrow, the air grows more stifling, the sight becomes clouded and the stench is awful. At one point, Dante says,

> Plumb in the middle of the dreadful cone
> > There yawns a well, exceeding deep and wide,
> > Whose form and fashion shall be told anon.
>
> That which remains, then, of the foul Pit's side,
> > Between the well and the foot of the craggy steep,
> > Is a narrowing round, which ten great chasms divide.
>
> > > (*Hell*, canto xviii)

Not only is the spiral downward in terms of the space, it is a regression away from the exchanges of shared love to an increasingly solitary and destructive imprisonment.

In Circle Two, Dante encounters a man and woman who tell a tale of their tender love affair. Francesca was engaged to marry Paolo's invalided brother, but as Paolo and Francesca lingered together, reading the story of Sir Lancelot and Guinevere, they ended up making love to each other.

> As we read on, our eyes met now and then,
> > And to our cheeks the changing color started,
> > But just one moment overcame us — when
>
> We read of the smile, desired of lips long thwarted
> > Such smile, by such a lover kissed away,
> > He that may never more from me be parted
>
> Trembling all over, kissed my mouth. I say
> > The book was Galleot, Galleot the complying
> > Ribald who wrote; we read no more that day.
>
> > > (*Hell*, canto v)

Dante faints with pity at the tale of their love. He does not have the expected hierarchy of sin. Adultery is put at the beginning of hell. By itself, it still shows the signs of adoration and mutual delight.[46] It is the lingering and the clinging that lands them in this place of being stuck with each other forever.

Dante descends from there to the realm of the gluttons. Here the enjoyment of mutual exchange has degenerated to solitary desire (I want what I want for myself). Below the gluttons are the misers, miserably attached to their addictions. They are unable even to enjoy their passionate clinging.

Going deeper still, Dante depicts those wallowing in self-pity and wrath. Passion has degenerated from mutuality to aloneness, to miserable self-centeredness and is beginning to erupt into violence.

Anger and hatred, as Dante graphically depicts, can be an outright fight or the deep resentments portrayed by those souls who lay buried in the mud and whose cries bubble up to the surface in incoherent froth.

> And I, staring about with eyes intent,
>   Saw mud-stained figures in the mire beneath,
>   Naked, with looks of savage discontent,
>
> At fisticuffs — not with fists alone, but with
>   Their head and heels, and with their bodies too,
>   And tearing each other piecemeal with their teeth.
>
> "Son," the kind master said, "here may'st thou view
>   The souls of those who yielded them to wrath;
>   Further, I'd have thee know and hold for true
>
> That others lie plunged deep in this vile broth,
>   Whose sighs — see there, wherever one may look —
>   Come bubbling up to the top and make it froth."
>
> (*Hell,* canto vii)

I must invite you to read the unfolding drama for yourself! From these sins Dante moves to the deeper sins of violence. Here, for example, are the heretics. We will not necessarily agree with Dante's specific examples, but the progression of untransformed passion is clear.

Heresy is not so much false doctrine in opposition to institutional religion. It is the loss of touch with reality, the natural consequence of a downward spiral into one's own addiction.

The heretics are those who begin to see the world through their compulsion. Their view is colored by the demand to have what they want. In order to justify their addiction, they have concluded that they have a corner on the truth and no one can challenge them. It is a defensive attachment to one's own illusions which poisons one's entire perception. It is this adamant clinging to one's own illusions that is so violent and destructive to others.

The possibility of relationship, of communication, and of trying to work together to make the relationship work is cut off. Now, regardless of the cost, the "heretic" is committed to a personal perception of reality. This, of course, is the self-deception so common in extramarital affairs. The marriage is finally destroyed not simply because of the affair, but because of the simultaneous refusal to confront reality.

Finally, Dante approaches the lower reaches of hell. It is fascinating to discover that there is almost no fire in Dante's hell. The bottom of hell is not a pit of fire but a frozen lake. All mutual enjoyment and celebration is gone. Here, in the words of Dorothy Sayers, is "a cold and cruel egotism, gradually striking inward till even the lingering passions of hatred and destruction are frozen into immobility."[47]

> And when we'd left him, in that icy bed,
>   I saw two frozen together in one hole
>   So that the one head capped the other head;
>
> And as starved men tear bread, this tore the poll
>   Of the one beneath, chewing with ravenous jaw,
>   Where brain meets marrow, just beneath the skull.
>
> (*Hell*, canto xxxii)

What a horrible picture. Of course we do not want to look at such an image. But we need to. We need to see the destructive power of our own refusals.

Many marriages can be described no better than the frozen state of two people gnawing on each other. As I write this, I recall the movie *The War of the Roses*. It describes the degeneration of a marriage — two people move from going their separate ways to choosing divorce to becoming so engrossed in their own interpretation of each other's responses and so paranoid of what the other is scheming that it ends in a conflagration of violence. Surely that is a Dantean description of hell.

The message is quite clear. Two things are at work here. The first is that the refusal to allow our passion to challenge our dependencies takes one into increasingly constricted and destructive experience. The second is that the affirmation of passion includes not only the celebration of the goodness of life, it also includes a stripping process.

Many people I talk to do not want to go on this journey. It appears that everything will be lost, that their world is getting narrower and narrower. It is like mucking around in the garbage. Surely we have better things to do than that.

I do not blame them. Most of us do not choose this experience voluntarily. We are pushed into it through the pain of our own disappointments and failures. But once on the way, Dante's hell stands like a beacon from a far away shore. We are reassured that the introspection necessary for healing is not just another contemporary neurosis. We can look across the centuries and see another light pointing in the same direction. The trip may not be pleasant, but it has integrity.

This honesty becomes one of the first indications of the transformation into health. Can we admit that in our determination to live passionately we so easily fixate on the object of our passion in such a way that our focus becomes increasingly narrow and eventually asphyxiating? Can we see the destructive results of these dependencies?

I have on my desk an inscription that was given to me by someone who comes for spiritual direction. It reads, "And then the day came when the pain it took to hang on became much greater than the pain it took to let go."[48]

18

Purgatory: The Journey into Freedom of Choice

PURGATORY, Dorothy Sayers says, "with its freshness, sparkle, and gaiety, its tenderness, its journeying in hope, and its reunion of true lovers after estrangement and separation, is the very stuff of fairy-tale and quintessence of all the romances."[49]

The journey recounted in *Purgatory* actually begins at the end of the volume *Hell*. In the final canto of that volume Dante reaches the lowest point in hell at the center of the earth. Then having passed the center point, he begins to ascend toward the surface of the earth on the opposite side of the world, "back to the lit world from the darkened dens" (*Hell*, canto xxxiv). Dante follows the course of a stream, the river Lethe, which is the river of forgetting or oblivion, but since he is traveling upstream he is traveling toward remembrance, toward honesty, and toward choice.

Purgatory, in Dante's vision, is pictured as a mountain, formed by the hollowing out of hell at the fall of Lucifer. It is the same mountain that Dante saw in the distance, so inviting yet so inaccessible, at the beginning of his journey.

As *Purgatory* opens, Dante is with Virgil on a boat approaching the mountain. His exhilaration is immense. The sun is shining, the air is fresh, and the color of the sky brilliant. He has literally returned to his senses. It is a totally different world. And although it will be an uphill climb, it is a place of creativity and hope.

> For to the second realm I tune my tale,
>> Where human spirits purge themselves, and train
>> To leap up into joy celestial.

> *(Purgatory,* canto i)

Dante's ascent to the top of a mountain signifies not only movement toward heaven but also purposeful and, at times, arduous work. We do not slide into healing. Recovery must be chosen and must be won. Hell was the first step of honesty. But hell is honesty without hope, acknowledgement without choice. Honesty alone is not enough. Honesty must give way to change and growth.

Merely describing our addictions can be as much of an evasion as denying them. As long as we can get by with naming our addictions we do not have to do anything about them. It is a major turning point in one's healing to move from honesty to choice.

I learned early in life that if I named my own struggles, I not only preempted other people's critique, I could look as if I was actually growing. One of these struggles has been my fear of taking initiative and asserting my will in the face of potential conflict. I could go on naming my problem forever, but that would not bring me to healing.

As Dante and Virgil reach the shore at the base of the mountain, the two travelers are met by Cato. Cato, in Roman history, was famous for his choice to commit suicide rather than lose his freedom.[50] He challenges their way, and Virgil replies on Dante's behalf,

> Be gracious to his coming, I entreat;
>> Tis liberty he seeks — how dear a thing
>> That is, they know who give their lives for it.

> *(Purgatory,* canto ii)

In that one plea lies the entire movement of *Purgatory*. Whatever Dante experiences, it is for the purpose of freedom. He is learning to choose, learning to honor his own passion and refusing to be a slave to it.

The Ascent of Purgatory

The first steps of the ascent are steep and exhausting, as though the gravity on the lower slopes pulls with greater force. It pictures for us those first few steps toward healing as the most difficult and the most exhausting. The choice to go for help, to challenge a life-long family pattern, to see a counselor, to join a twelve-step group — these seem almost beyond one's ability. Everything conspires to suck one back down into the old patterns.

Just before reaching the gate of purgatory, Dante falls asleep exhausted. While he is asleep, a lady named Lucy carries him up the last ascent to the gate.

> A lady came: "I am Lucy" — thus she said;
>   "Come, let me take this sleeper; I've a mind
>   To help him on the road he has to tread."

(Purgatory, canto ix)

It is a tender picture of the grace that underlies the entire journey. During the struggle to come to healing it will often feel as though we are totally alone. The hard work seems never-ending. "I'm tired of growing!" is a complaint that I often hear as I listen to people.

It is the gift of grace from his "Higher Power," when Lucy carries him. This alone enables Dante to reach the gate of choice toward healing. That carrying power will be there, invisibly, with Dante throughout the climb. No one can do it alone. It is the quiet, reassuring presence of our Higher Power that provides the necessary strength to keep going.

After entering the gate, the ascent up the mountain of purgatory, toward the earthly paradise at the top, is divided into three series of terraces. In each of these sections a different cluster of distorted passion is dealt with. Just as the descent into hell was away from exchanges of love into isolation, the ascent up the mountain moves from isolation back into shared love.

In the lowest section the struggle with pride, envy, and wrath are purged. These appear to be the exact opposite of love. There is no exchange; they are solitary experiences. Dante does not depict them as devoid of love, but so twisted in love that the passion expresses itself in harm to others in order to assert oneself.

In the second section, midway up the mountain, sloth is purged. Sloth is not a word we use much anymore. We associate it with laziness. But the concept was richer for Dante. Sloth was seen by Dante as the failure to pursue the passion of love fully.

> If to the vision and the quest you've given
> But lukewarm love....

> (*Purgatory*, canto xvii)

Sloth is the fear of passion. It is the paralysis that comes through choosing to avoid or protect oneself from passion.

Many are simply too afraid. They would rather remain in a comfortable but sterile rut than contend with passion. They are afraid of being out of control, afraid that passion will overwhelm them. "Give me security and rules." And not only do they want these boundaries for themselves, they expect others to fit into them too!

Sloth must be purged. It may be safe but it does not lead to life. It does not harm others intentionally but neither does it risk living.

Here at this midway point up the mountain and central to understanding *Purgatory*, Dante pauses for a discussion with Virgil on the nature of love. Dante is told that love is at the root of all these sins. Love, he says, energizes our passion whether it is expressed in constructive or destructive ways.

> Bethink thee then how love must be the seed
> In you, not only of each virtuous action,
> But also of each punishable deed.

> (*Purgatory*, canto xvii)

Then in the next canto Dante asks,

> Wherefore, my kindest, dearest Father, please
>   Define me love, to which thou dost reduce
>   All virtuous actions and their contraries.

> *(Purgatory,* canto xviii)

Virgil replies that love is the yearning awakened the moment we see something outside ourselves we desire. It appears so beautiful, so potent. Virgil says that in the moment of seeing a more profound glory is revealed, an "inward image." Whether we know it or not, we have seen a glimpse of God present in the object of our desire. The pleasure encountered in that moment fuels the yearning into a longing for union. This yearning, Virgil says, is the love that binds the entire universe together.

> The soul, which is created apt for love,
>   The moment pleasure wakes it into act,
>   To any pleasant thing is swift to move.

> Your apprehension draws from some real fact
>   An inward image, which it shows to you,
>   And by that image doth the soul attract:

> And if the soul, attracted, yearns thereto,
>   That yearning's love: 'tis nature doth secure
>   Her bond in you, which pleasure knits anew.

> *(Purgatory,* canto xviii)

Virgil continues by saying that this passion of love must find direction if it is to be whole. Reason gives direction to the passion through the exercise of free choice. It is the "counsellor-power" that blends with passion to bring about constructive choice.

> Now, to keep all volitions else well blent
>   With this, you have a counsellor-power innate
>   Set there to guard the threshold of assent:

> They who by reasoning probed creation's plan
>   Root-deep, perceived this inborn liberty
>   And bequeathed ethics to the race of man.

> Grant, then, all loves that wake in you to be
> Born of necessity, you still possess
> Within yourselves the power of mastery;

(Purgatory, canto xviii)

This is an incredible affirmation. We often try to deal with our destructive choices by containing them or suppressing them. Not only are the actions unacceptable to us, the impulse behind them is unacceptable too. We seek to hide the pride or squelch the lust.

What are we to do when we experience passion and especially passion for that which we know would be destructive to pursue? What do we do with the seductive power of addictions? Dante suggests in *Purgatory* that the distorted passion is purged by uncovering the truth of love at the heart of the impulse and by setting that passion free for the good.

Dante calls it a love "born of necessity." We do not choose when or about what we will be passionate, but he reminds us that we still have the power of choice. Strong words! Accepting the passion of love includes the choice to order the passion to its truest end.

This is the reconciliation between passion and intellect. In the end a tremendous creative power will be his. Intellect will inform the direction of his choice and passion will inflame the power of his choice. He will be empowered to live in the freedom of healed love.

As Dante moves on toward the top of the mountain, he encounters the third series of terraces of Purgatory where the struggle with excessive love is dealt with. Here Dante encounters the covetous, the gluttons, and the lustful.

As in hell, these are, in Dante's scheme, closer to the glory of love's exchange. They have embraced the passion, what they now need is discretion. As they revel in the strength of their passion AND exercise their choice for the good, they will discover freedom. They will be enabled to see the full beauty of the presence of God in the object of their longing and in the longing itself.

Throughout the journey up the mountain, Dante describes each of these distortions of love in the process of being healed. He does not expect us to focus equally on each sin. None of us struggles with all of them. We each have our preferred ways in which we distort love.

What he does, through the experiences at each terrace, is to suggest ways of meditating or praying with these struggles and of opening them up for healing. Dante encounters at each new terrace a series of images, examples, and particular prayers. Each of these aids meditation. Each provides a way to let go of demand without letting go of the passion.

The images of the proud doubled over carrying heavy stones or the envious with their eyes sewn shut are there to aid in self aware-ness, the examples from history and scripture provide models both positive and negative for contemplation. The set prayers are like repetitive prayers that become part of one's psyche through con-stant use. The prayer themes acknowledge that we cannot do this on our own and bring together our choice for healing with God's gracious assistance to bring that healing to us.

Dante pictures people remaining in purgatory for a long time. Keeping in mind that he is projecting present experience into the afterlife, we see that Dante is dramatically picturing how long the struggle for wholeness really is.

There is a gradual process of self-recognition. We slowly choose to respond toward the good. And gradually there is a joining of our choice with the presence of grace provided for our help.

This kind of growth is not the result of one prayer or a new resolution. Freedom from any addictive experience is the discipline of a long process of growth. That is why Dante depicts these people sojourning in purgatory for long years. He is figuratively depicting the frequent feeling that growth toward freedom takes "forever."

The Earthly Paradise

The ascent of Purgatory ends at the top of the mountain, in the gar-den of the earthly paradise. The earthly paradise is the place where the divine and human find their highest earthly union. Freedom is gained where love is experienced in its fullness and seen in its true glory.

The central vision occurs in a grand revelation of Beatrice. Her appearance is startling. Dante describes the approach of a regal and majestic procession. His description consciously follows Ezekiel's description of the glory of God seen in the vision of the wheels.

Amazingly when the chariot arrives, it is Beatrice whom it carries. A picture of ineffable brightness unfolds as Dante describes the canopied carriage, the dancing and the color. He is leading us to anticipate, in the car of glorious triumph, the victorious Christ or a vision of God. Instead, he describes the appearance of Beatrice, that same woman who, so many years ago had made his heart stop with her beauty and beat again with his love.

> In a white veil beneath an olive-crown
> > Appeared to me a lady cloaked in green,
> > And living flame the colour of her gown;
>
> And instantly, for all the years between
> > Since her mere presence with a kind of fright
> > Could awe me and make my spirit faint within,
>
> There came on me, needing no further sight,
> > Just by that strange, outflowing power of hers,
> > The old, old love in all its mastering might.

> (*Purgatory,* canto xxx)

It is a stunning revelation! Certainly for Dante. Maybe more so for us! Here the human and the divine converge. After all the long process of healing, the culminating experience is the young "puppy love" reemerging in all its original explosive force. The seeing and the desiring of Dante as a child have been brought to full fruition.

In the final lines of *Purgatory,* the newly revealed Beatrice confronts Dante with his past failures in love. For a moment it seems as though the revelation of the glory of love will only become another means of reproach. We might fear that to discover how potent each exchange in life is, how full of God and full of love our world is will only discourage us. Who can ever live up to it?

The revelation of Beatrice as the bearer of God to Dante cannot help but be, in some way, a judgment on all the lesser experiences. Dante is called to a "fearless moral inventory." Then *Purgatory* closes with Dante's encounter with two bodies of water.

Immediately he is drawn into the river Lethe, the river he had followed out of hell. While he is almost in a faint with horror at his failure in love, he is plunged into the stream of forgetting. Then later, he is invited to drink from another river, the river Eunoe which means "good remembrance."

What might have been discouraging to Dante, now becomes the means of great grace. In his encounter with Beatrice, Dante finds that the painful memory of all the past failures disappears. The terrible reminder of broken dreams and lost love and failed opportunities is gone. Dante will still remember his past, but not with a sense of failure. He will see, even in his past mistakes, the good that has been part of his journey to this place of healing.

The mystery of love reveals that love is present in distorted passion and in our failures and losses. Dante discovers that all of his experiences, even the broken ones, have been incorporated into his recovery of love.

19

Paradise:
The Journey
into Mystical Oneness

JUST as *Purgatory* opens with a complete change of atmosphere from *Hell*, in *Paradise* the atmosphere is changed from freshness and hopefulness to one of mystery and even caution.

Dante is embarking on the most difficult part of the whole epic. It is much easier to write good poetry about the grotesqueness of hell or the struggle of purgatory than to describe the goodness of paradise.

Dante is going to penetrate through the glory of the image, whether of Beatrice or a beautiful sunset, to pursue the encounter with God that is promised in the image itself.

In Dante's own experience, the glory encountered in Beatrice, and the adoration of that glory, brings him into a mystery that is beyond him. In the opening canto he hints at the sense of mystery and caution; in the second he expounds it.

With a touch of satire, he suggests that if we are interested in pursuing the mystery of love only for its poetic or entertainment value ("for the song's sake"), we better turn our little cockle-shell boats back. We are in too deep for curiosity.

> O you that follow in light cockle-shells,
>   For the song's sake, my ship that sails before,
>   Carving her course and singing as she sails,
>
> Turn back and seek the safety of the shore;
>   Tempt not the deep, lest losing unawares
>   Me and yourselves, you come to port no more.

> (*Paradise*, canto ii)

Love and passion are meant to change one's life. If you follow, you must do so at the risk of being changed.

Paradise addresses the question, "If we are going to welcome passion without demanding fulfilment, what shall we do with the passion? Will it be like a loose cannon on the deck and will we be victims of its unannounced onslaught?" Dante's answer is that passion freed from addictive attachments is the emerging energy by which we come into deepest communion with God, the Center of all things.

This penetration to the Source may happen in one moment and then be gone. It may happen on a hike in the woods or over coffee with a friend. It is not a permanent state. But when it is gone, our vision is changed, and our capacity to delight in and adore all of life is increased.

Three major themes run through *Paradise*. The first is wonder. By using the metaphor of burning light, Dante is emphasizing the incredible awe we discover in those mystical experiences of the divine glory.

The second theme is wholeness that comes from the union or integration of all of who we are. Dante speaks of "intellect drawing close to desire." We are approaching the restoration of wholeness. We could add today the welcoming of our body-self.

The third theme is empowerment. In Dante's concept, will is the energizing power that draws all things to the good. This power is initially indicated by the phrase "who moves all things." All three of these themes are gathered together in the opening lines:

The glory of Him who moves all things so'er
  Impenetrates the universe, and bright
  The splendour burns, more here and lesser there.

Within that heav'n which most receives His light
  Was I, and saw such things as man nor knows
  Nor skills to tell, returning from that height.

For when our intellect is drawing close
  To its desire, its paths are so profound
  That memory cannot follow where it goes.

(Paradise, canto i)

Wonder

Dante acknowledges that there is a variety in the way the world reveals its inherent glory. Not all glories have the same intensity. Not every experience of love reveals the total glory; not every moment of wonder is equally profound.

To believe as we enter life that we will truly experience the presence of God around us does not mean that we will be overcome with a sense of mystical awe everywhere. But it does mean that all things share in some measure that awesome presence.

The beauty of freely exchanged love can be discerned anywhere from a little flicker to the center of all lights in the direct presence of God. Therefore there is a progression in *Paradise* from the true but distant light of partially revealed glory to the blinding direct vision of God at the center of all things. Dante gradually becomes aware of and accustomed to the light.

Dante is expressing through the metaphor that, as we allow our sensual experience to point us to the presence of God, we become increasingly sensitive to God present everywhere.

Later in the same opening canto, Dante illustrates what he means. As he and Beatrice prepare to ascend above the earth, she is able to look directly at the sun, but he is not. Dante looks at the brightness by gazing at Beatrice instead. Yet in that very act of adoring the reflected glory in her face he experiences a transformation (Dante coins a word translated here "transhumanized").

> Beatrice stood, her eyes still riveted
> > On the eternal wheels; and, constantly,
> > Turning mine thence, I gazed on her instead;
>
> 'Twas even thus a change came over me,
> > As Glaucus, eating of the weed, changed race
> > And grew a god among the gods of sea.
>
> *Transhumanized* — the fact mocks human phrase;
> > So let the example serve, till proof requite
> > Him who is called to experience this by grace.
>
> > > > (*Paradise*, canto i)

This is the gradual awakening of Dante to the glory. In the language of the Apostle Paul, by gazing into the image of Christ we are transformed into the same image.

T. S. Eliot describes the same process in *The Four Quartets*. He speaks of hints of glory in a garden. By looking into the pool he can see the reflection of great Presences behind him. However, almost as soon as he sees it, a cloud passes over and the image is gone. We have moments of mystical experience, but just moments. He adds, "humankind cannot bear very much reality."[51]

Wholeness

Secondly, these mystical experiences of glory bring to us the recovery of wholeness through the integration of reason and passion. It is a merging of energy and choice. Reason enables one to get beyond attachment to the image itself through choice.

Reason then begins to give way to imagination. Imagination points us beyond what we can actually think about because it does not need definition. It is almost like dreaming. But eventually even imagination fails. In the final approach to God Dante says, "high phantasy lost power and here broke off" (canto xxxiii).

There is in the very nature of mystical experience a built-in limitation to intellect. Now intellect must rely on the energy of passion to take it deeper into the mystery.

Empowerment

Finally, the experience of union brings about empowerment. In the opening lines of *Paradise,* God is described as the One who moves all things.

Looking up at the stars and planets, we can see a vast movement of rotation. It becomes for Dante a picture of empowered choice. In the place of purified love, all things are drawn together and choose to move harmoniously in a dance, energized by love.

In the wholeness that comes through the liberation of love, people are empowered to reenter the dance floor and dance in intimacy with the whole world. Love is the inner dynamism that energizes the universe. It enflames all with glory and moves all. In it, the spheres of existence whirl.

We are invited to join with the power of all things and become co-creators with God. We are called to creativity and power. How is that to be accomplished? As reason guides passion toward the Center of all things and then loses itself in the passionate penetration into God, we join the great wheeling universe. Love becomes power within the mystical unity, power to move in harmony with the universe.

We will not trace the entire progression through *Paradise.* In that journey Dante, using the personalities and events both of his own time and that of history, seeks to express what a love-empowered will might look like. What looms largest for Dante is his sense of justice. When passion is owned and healed, the creative power of justice within human society becomes a possibility.

It is a theme that takes on a monumental importance in our world. The world can no longer afford private visions of healing and the recovery of love. We may not agree exactly with Dante's examples. We may see, for example, our sense of justice more democratic and Dante's more monarchical. Yet Dante reminds us clearly that the recovery of love is not an individualistic thing. It is a personal journey but it has enormous social implications.

Dante saw in the collapse of the major social structures of his day a necessary call. It did not produce in him a sense of victimization, but a call to empowered action. He saw that the journey into love would encompass the very social struggles that were inherent in the collapse of the Roman Empire and the church. To live love is to love justice, the prophet tells us (Mic. 6:8).

The Final Experience of God at the Center

In the closing cantos of *Paradise* Dante moves toward the very presence of God at the hub of all things. In canto xxviii, Dante begins the transition from indirect contemplation of God to direct sight.

He says that by looking with love into the eyes of Beatrice he catches sight of a reflected light. He turns to look and in turning sees God directly for the first time.

> . . . While I was gazing into the lovely eyes
> Wherewith Love made a noose to capture me;

> . . . as I turned, there greeted mine likewise
> What all behold who contemplate aright
> That heaven's revolutions through the skies.

> One Point I saw, so radiantly bright,
> So searing to the eyes it strikes upon,
> They needs must close before such piercing light.

> *(Paradise,, canto xxviii)*

Then after seeing all creation in relationship to this single "Point" of light, Beatrice and Dante move closer. She says,

> . . . We have won beyond the worlds, and move
> Within that heaven which is pure light alone:

> Pure intellectual light, fulfilled with love,
> Love of the true Good, filled with all delight,
> Transcending sweet delight, as sweets above.

> *(Paradise, canto xxx)*

Beatrice then leaves Dante in the company of Bernard (St. Bernard of Clairvaux whose mysticism was filled with erotic love). Bernard keeps pointing Dante toward the central light. Dante discerns the integration of all things, even those experiences that seem so scattered and trivial. Here our whole being is "fused" with all things.

> In that abyss I saw how love held bound
>> Into one volume all the leaves whose flight
>> Is scattered through the universe around;
>
> How substance, accident and mode unite
>> Fused, so to speak, together in such wise
>> That this I tell of is one simple light.
>
>> *(Paradise,* canto xxxiii)

As he continues to gaze, Dante sees within the center of the light the form of three yet one. In the middle of this vision of the Trinity, he makes out the presence of Jesus in human form.

This is the final vindication of the moment of passion way back at the party when Dante was nine years old. Humanity is never lost. In Dante's spiritual awakening the physical and sensual are never superseded. In the words of the ancient creed, our humanity has been taken into God.

> But as my sight by seeing learned to see,
>> The transformation which in me took place
>> Transformed the single changeless form for me.
>
> That light supreme, within its fathomless
>> Clear substance, showed to me three spheres, which bare
>> Three hues distinct, and occupied one space;
>
> ... The sphering thus begot, perceptible
>> In Thee like mirrored light, now to my view —
>> When I had looked on it a little while —
>
> Seemed in itself, and in its own self-hue,
>> Limned with our image; for which cause mine eyes
>> Were altogether drawn and held thereto.
>
>> *(Paradise,* canto xxxiii)

Dante has reached the final point. He sees. But there is more than sight, there is actual union. As he struggles to integrate the impossibility of human image occupying the divine Center ("how to fit the image to the sphere"), he himself becomes one with what he sees. Passion breaks through beyond words and imagination. Dante's own will and desire are unified and become part of the wheeling of the universe as it is moved by love.

> So strove I with that wonder — how to fit
>> The image to the sphere; so sought to see
>> How it maintained the point of rest in it.
>
> Thither my own wings could not carry me,
>> But that a flash my understanding clove,
>> Whence its desire came to it suddenly.
>
> High phantasy lost power and here broke off;
>> Yet, as a wheel moves smoothly, free from jars,
>> My will and my desire were turned by love,
>
> The love that moves the sun and the other stars.

> (*Paradise*, canto xxxiii)

Dante has reached the final goal of union with all things through love. The mystical moment may only last for five seconds and then be irretrievably gone, but it is his forever.

These are the moments that inform our lives and move us to keep opening to love. They are the seeming accidents, the wonderful ambushes that remind us that there is more. They bring the empowering of union so that our whole being is one with the creative energy of the universe.

Abraham Heschel, with whose words we began this section, speaks of the faith produced in these moments. His words haunt me in the irresistible search for my own recovery of love.

> Faith is not the clinging to a shrine but an endless pilgrimage of the heart. Audacious longing, burning songs, daring thoughts, an impulse overwhelming the heart, usurping the mind — these are all a drive toward [loving the One] who rings our hearts like a bell.[52]

Conclusion

Is love a possibility in our world? Is the vision too large? Too difficult? Will the passion that confronts us be too much for us? Is it unfair to encourage people to pursue love?

My heart is full as I write these words. These are the questions I wrestle with at night and in my own moments of discouragement. I sometimes wish there were some other, some safer way to recover love.

I keep returning, despite my protestations, to the conviction that the recovery of love is not an option. Thomas Merton once said, "Try your best not to become a monk!" But sometimes there is little choice. One thing I do know, this vision of love cannot be seen as a standard by which we are to evaluate ourselves. It would be devastating.

Those who have already begun the journey to recovery will recognize at least parts of the vision offered by these writers. They will be familiar with some of the signposts and landmarks. The vision of love presented will be confirming and broadening for those people. Those who are beginning to discover the journey can receive permission and encouragement to continue on the way.

Recovering a positive vision of love is a lifetime of challenge. It is not a sentimental way to maintain a positive view of the world. Nor is it an escape from the realities of our broken experience. It is Reality.

Love is the soil of our lives, the energy of our existence, and the goal of all our longings. It is this vast panorama, witnessed to by these writers, that can inspire us in our recovery from the bruised and shattered experiences of our addictions and dysfunctional patterns.

149

Each of the four mystics of the fourteenth century has addressed an important part of that vision of love. Their struggle is our struggle, and their vision can become ours.

We have seen through the book the gradual building of a framework for living with our own passion in life. That framework opens the universe up to us, giving us wide vistas of possibility.

It is as though they have presented to us a grand stage play. Julian of Norwich has provided the stage and the props. The entire universe, loved into being and held in love, is the backdrop.

The world in which we live is energized and sustained in love. Love is the essence, deeper than all the brokenness we experience. The universe is a friendly place and we can risk opening up to love.

John Ruusbroec has announced the plot of this great play. More than any other writer, he has shown us the dimensions of love by taking us to the heart of all things in the Trinity. There he described the passionate tension between our cravings for union and for individuality.

The love that informs the universe is a storm of longing in which there is constant passion to experience both the uniqueness of personhood and the joy of union. The tension between these two simultaneous realities gives to love its energy and its mystery. It is an unfathomable craving to consume and to be consumed, to stand alone and to be oned.

In the play of love, Meister Eckhart and Dante Alighieri give us virtuoso performances of the two central roles. Eckhart brings us face to face with our need to live at home with ourselves. It is a long passage home because we have gone out of ourselves so easily in our search for meaning.

Especially in our consumer culture we have been tricked into thinking that life is to be found outside us and not within. In coming back to our center we go beyond our brokenness and beyond ego to the mystery of union with God in our very ground.

Finally, Dante invites us to union through the affirmation of God's presence in the world around us. Celebration of the divine presence through adoration frees the passion and fuels our movement into oneness with the divine Life which moves all things.

There is obviously a lifetime of experiences to be faced in learning to live out this vision. The vision provides direction rather than answers.

In the middle of the next uncertainty as to how to live love, how will one be able to decide what is the best choice? A positive vision of love gives the signposts. It reassures us that the world, for all its troubles, is still safe enough for us to open up and live passionately. It reminds us that it is important to be passionate about life. It validates the experience of love even if that comes to us in unsuspecting ways.

But at the same time, this vision points the way to freedom in love through the transformation of desire. It does not allow us to live a cheap form of love. The recovery of love is the means of our salvation.

$\mathcal{N}otes$

Preface

1. Walter Brueggemann, *The Prophetic Imagination* (Philadelphia: Fortress Press, 1978).

2. I do not claim to be an expert on the fourteenth century or on the writers introduced here. There will obviously be oversimplification. But there is also, I trust, perceptive enough insight to validate their contributions to our study.

Part I: Meeting of Two Worlds

3. Thomas Merton, *Spiritual Direction and Meditation* (Wheathampstead, England: Anthony Clarke Books, 1950), 17.

4. Evelyn Underhill, *Practical Mysticism* 1915; reprint (Columbus: Ariel Press, n.d.), 23.

5. Barbara Tuchman, *A Distant Mirror* (New York: Ballantine Books, 1978).

6. See Thomas Howard, *Chance or the Dance* (Wheaton, IL: Harold Shaw Publishers, 1969), 13ff.

7. Aquinas was neither the first nor the only Christian theologian to use the categories of Aristotle. He was simply the greatest and therefore the best known.

Part II: Julian of Norwich: The Environment of Love and the Healing of Trust

8. Gabriele Uhlein, *Meditations with Hildegard of Bingen* (Santa Fe: Bear & Co., 1982), 52.

9. Sue Woodruff, *Meditations with Mechtild of Magdeburg* (Santa Fe: Bear & Co., 1982), 27.

10. James Houston, *Transforming Friendship* (Oxford: Lion Books, 1989), and Matthew Fox, *The Coming of the Cosmic Christ* (San Francisco: Harper & Row, 1988); both mention the question posed to Einstein without giving a reference.

11. M. H. Abrams, ed., *Norton Anthology of English Literature* (New York: W. W. Norton & Co., 1975), 1816.

12. See Henri Nouwen's excellent discussion of fear-based experience in *Lifesigns* (New York: Image Books, 1986), 15–24.

13. This is the more common title of Julian's work. The text used in this book uses the title *Showings*.

14. Thomas Merton, *Conjectures of a Guilty Bystander* (New York: Doubleday and Co., 1966), 275.

15. Underhill, *Practical Mysticism*, 136, 137.

16. See James Finley's *Merton's Palace of Nowhere* (Notre Dame: Ave Maria Press, 1978), for an excellent discussion of the true and false self in Thomas Merton's writings.

Part III: John Ruusbroec: Love and Passion

17. T. S. Eliot, *The Four Quartets: Little Gidding*, pt. 4, lines 207–213.

18. John Ruusbroec, *The Spiritual Espousals and Other Works* (New York: Paulist Press, 1985), 171.

19. Evelyn Underhill, *Mysticism* 1955; reprint (New York: New American Library, 1974), 422.

20. Evelyn Underhill, *Mystics of the Church* (Cambridge: James Clarke & Co., 1925), 148.

21. *New Catholic Encyclopedia*, s.v. "Ruysbroeck,"

22. Ernesto Cardenal, *To Live Is to Love* (Garden City, NY: Image Books, 1974).

Part IV: Meister Eckhart: Coming Home to Ourselves

23. Gerald May, *Addiction and Grace* (San Francisco: Harper & Row, 1988), 181.

24. Robert Bly, trans., *Selected Poems of Rainer Maria Rilke* (New York: Harper & Row, 1981), 4.

25. Rowan Williams, *The Wound of Knowledge*, rev. ed. (London: Darton, Longman and Todd Ltd., 1990), 132ff.

26. Edmund College and Bernard McGinn, *Meister Eckhart: The Essential Sermons, Commentaries, Treatises and Defense* (New York: Paulist Press, 1981), 14, 15.

27. Robin Norwood, *Women Who Love Too Much* (Los Angeles: J. P. Tarcher, 1985).

28. Scott Peck, *The Different Drum* (New York: Simon and Schuster, 1987), 188ff.

29. *The Cloud of Unknowing,* trans. Clifton Wolters (Middlesex: Penguin Books, 1961), 55.

30. "Isness" is the translators' way of describing the use of the Latin, *esse,* that is central to Eckhart's thought. See the introduction in the volume by College and McGinn used as the text here and its companion volume, Bernard McGinn, *Meister Eckhart: Teacher and Preacher* (New York: Paulist Press, 1986). Eckhart is always careful in the end to distinguish that although we truly participate in God, God is always utterly more.

31. See the incredibly touching characterization of this dilemma in Eliot, *The Four Quartets: East Coker,* pt. 5, lines 172–209.

32. Elizabeth O'Connor, *Cry Pain, Cry Hope* (Waco, TX: Word Books, 1987), 49.

33. Edmund Colledge, trans., *Mediaeval Netherlands Religious Literature* (London: London House, 1965), 56.

34. May, *Addiction and Grace,* 167.

35. Houston, *Transforming Friendship,* 219.

36. Tilden Edwards, *Spiritual Friendship* (New York: Paulist Press, 1980), 145.

Part V: Dante Alighieri: The Glory of Passionate Exchange

37. In Samuel Dresner, ed., *I Asked for Wonder* (New York: Crossroad, 1985), 17.

38. Charles Williams, *The Figure of Beatrice: A Study in Dante* (New York: Octagon Books, 1980), 109.

39. Anthony de Mello, *Awareness* (New York: Doubleday, 1990), 27.

40. Barbara Reynolds, trans., *La Vita Nuova* (Middlesex: Penguin, 1969), 30.

41. The *Convivio* was actually begun after his exile had begun.

42. Anthony de Mello, *The Song of the Bird* (New York: Image Books, 1984), 2.

43. May, *Addiction and Grace,* 1.

44. William McNamara, *Mystical Passion: Spirituality for a Bored Society* (New York: Paulist Press, 1977), 10.

45. Williams, *The Figure of Beatrice,* 146. In his characteristically dense way, Williams wrote, "It [i.e., the soul that wills or, as we would say, the person] must cease to know the Images as *it* chooses; it must know them as they are; that is, as God chose them to be; that is, it must (in its degree) know them as God knows them in their union with him."

46. Williams, *The Figure of Beatrice,* 118. Williams makes the incisive

comment, "The formal sin here is the adultery of the two lovers; the poetic sin is their shrinking from the adult love demanded of them, and their refusal of the opportunity of glory . . . the sin is possible to all lovers, married or unmarried, adulterous or marital."

47. Dorothy Sayers, trans., *The Comedy of Dante Alighieri: Hell* (Middlesex, England: Penguin, 1949), 275.

48. I do not know the source of this quotation.

49. Dorothy Sayers, trans., *The Comedy of Dante Alighieri: Purgatory* (Middlesex, England: Penguin, 1955), 19.

50. James Collins, *Pilgrim in Love: An Introduction to Dante and His Spirituality* (Chicago: Loyola University Press, 1984), 121.

51. T. S. Eliot, *The Four Quartets: Burnt Norton,* Part 1, lines 42, 43.

52. Heschel, in Dresner, ed., 15. I have substituted "loving the One" for "serving Him."